The LOVING TRUTH *About* MONEY

The LOVING TRUTH *About* MONEY

A Practical Guide to Creating Financial Peace

DIANA RICHEY

ATHENA BOOKS

Published by Athena Books, LLC, Jackson, Wyoming
https://dianarichey.com

Edited and designed by Girl Friday Productions
www.girlfridayproductions.com

Cover design: Greg Mortimer
Project management: Sara Spees Addicott
Editorial production: Reshma Kooner

ISBN (paperback): 979-8-9909058-0-1
ISBN (ebook): 979-8-9909058-1-8

Printed in the United States.

Library of Congress Control Number: 2025905666

First edition

To you, the reader. May you find true authenticity and wild abundance.

CONTENTS

INTRODUCTION

This may be the most disjointed book you'll ever read. It's a personal finance book. And when I started this project, I felt called to create a one-stop-shop guide to personal finance. I wanted you to hold this book and feel a sense of peace, knowing that you had everything in your hands to thrive financially, once and for all. And this book certainly accomplishes that goal. It's comprehensive and complete, and everything is right here. But it's a strange book.

Part 2 is what you probably expect in a personal finance book. It's an overview of retirement accounts, tax-savvy savings strategies, and money management techniques.

Part 3 is perhaps more of a curveball. We talk about investing. But rather than telling you to put your money in a low-cost passive index fund, which is the advice du jour, we talk about how to select and value companies that align with your personal values and that are doing great things in the world.

But part 1 is where this book is really weird. We talk about how to craft the life of your dreams and earn the money you want doing what you love. And to get there, we have to dive deep. We have to get into the unseen—call it the spiritual, the energetic, the esoteric, the divine, Source, light, shadow, mother, father, consciousness, Buddha, Gaia, God. Whatever you want to call it, part 1 highlights some principles for working with and dancing with this Source energy. Worse yet, I don't have any rational or scientific proof for why these principles work. Unlike in part 2, where I can cite the US tax code, all I have for part 1 is evidence from my own life. And so part 1 of this book is a bit of woo-woo mixed with a bit of autobiography.

So there you have it. A personal finance book that hardly hangs together. But it's my best thinking on how to craft a life you love, and I offer it in the hope that it will help you thrive.

PART I

Creating

The first step of the financial planning process is to co-create the life of your dreams.

This probably seems like a strange and overly ambitious place to start. But I believe that financial planning is the art of creating your dream life. Typically, when we think of financial planning, we think about financial goals such as saving for retirement or college. We think about our income and our spending. And we think about how much we're saving and investing. But I think that definition misses the mark. According to most people I talk to, we don't really want money for the sake of having money. Instead, we want money so we don't have to think about money. We want to move through the world with freedom and ease. We want to feel peace and love and joy and connection. We don't want to have to worry about the price of groceries. We don't want to feel financial stress. We want to contribute to the world in a way that feels meaningful. We want sovereignty and autonomy. There are all sorts of things that we need to live a rich and fulfilling life. Money is a big one. Love is a big one. Health is a big one. So through-out part 1, we'll explore an approach to financial planning that doesn't just get you to retirement or get your kid through a pricey four-year college. We'll explore a definition of financial planning that helps you create the life of your dreams.

Um, how exactly? Legitimate question. Let's zoom out a bit first.

Let's assume that there are two approaches to life: the material approach and the spiritual approach. We'll call the material approach the *horizontal* approach, and the spiritual approach the *vertical* approach.

The material approach to life and money focuses on work, career, and action. It's a great approach. We work hard and get good grades in school. Maybe we're lucky enough to attend college or get some specialized training or education. And then we work in our chosen field. Maybe we join a big company or a small business or a midsize firm. Maybe we make art or music. Maybe we're self-employed. Maybe we start a company or become CEO of a Fortune 500. We grow, we get promoted, we hopefully make more money. We make phone calls, attend meetings, connect with customers, buy supplies, set up LLCs, write, analyze, present, teach. We make things happen. It's a very action-oriented energy, and this essence of *doing* is great.

But there are two potential pitfalls. Action-oriented en-ergy can become unbalanced. On one side of the ledger, a shortage of action can lead to complacency. We procrastinate. We don't take the steps that move us toward our goals. That's one imbalance. On the other side of the ledger, we push too hard. We go, go, go, go, go without ever thinking about where we're going. We look back on our lives and wonder what it was all for. We made money. We achieved financial security. We paid for retirement. But our spirits left a lot on the table. And in the shorter term, we battled stress, burnout, and adrenal fa-tigue. As we think about creating the life of our dreams in the material and horizontal, the aim is balance. We want to take action but also leave space for peace and joy.

The spiritual approach to life and money focuses on the inner work. We look inside to examine our strengths, our gifts, our shadows, and our blocks. We shed the things that aren't serving us. We take responsibility for the ways that we, consciously and unconsciously, contribute to our own misery and the misery of others. We go easy on ourselves. We move toward peace, love, and joy, and we are committed to growth, even though growth can feel hard.

These are good things—but, like the material approach, the spiritual approach can become unbalanced in one of two ways. On the one hand, we can lack faith and feel unsupported by the universe. We can fall into malaise or even depression when we believe that the issues in our lives are insurmountable and that trust and surrender are meaningless endeavors. Lacking faith, we never have the courage to start to peer inside. We roll around in our own suffering. On the other hand, there is the "pennies from heaven" approach. There is a whole bunch of literature and urban legend about spirituality and money. It goes something like this: I deserve abundance so I'm just going to sit here and wait for the sky to rain money on me. I am going to "think positive," repeat affirmations in the mirror, and pray for cash until I'm blue in the face. If you've tried any of these approaches, I probably don't have to tell you that the results are underwhelming.

So, what's the point? Why all this talk about vertical and horizontal? Working in the horizontal alone can be helpful. Working in the vertical alone can be helpful. But the real power comes in the "yes and" approach. By working in both the inner world and the outer world, we can make miracles happen.

If you're reading this personal finance book, it's entirely possible that your finances aren't quite what you'd like them to be. Maybe you're a little bit in debt. Maybe you're massively in debt. Maybe you'd like to make more money. Maybe you make great money but you're stuck in a career you hate. Maybe you've dedicated your life to parenting but want to build a professional life and make your own money. Maybe you depend on a partner for cash. Maybe you're recently divorced and trying to figure out how to put your life (and financial life) back together. The situations and money challenges we face come in innumerable flavors and colors. But money challenges all share that "eek" factor—as in "Eek! How am I going to solve this? In between glimmers of optimism, I feel guilty, ashamed, afraid, overwhelmed, down, and consumed by self-doubt."

So in part 1, we'll tell the story behind the story. We'll dive deep into the subject of energetics, which I think of as the language of the universe. You may have heard statements like "The universe has your back" or "The universe wants the best for you." I agree. Universal forces are pushing you toward a place of peace and balance, which includes abundance and financial well-being. The rub is that the universe uses not only things that we perceive as "good" but also things that we perceive as "bad" to help us grow. Like any good parent, the universe sometimes has to let bad things happen to help us learn. If we don't understand the universe's signs, signals, and language, then life can feel like random chaos that happens *to* us. But once we start to learn the universe's language—the language of energetics—then we become powerful co-creators. We understand that we have the power to create the life of our dreams.

Chapters 1 through 4 outline a four-step process for how to harness the power of energetics to create financial abundance and the life of your dreams. Chapter 5 offers a little case study on what it looks like to have all four steps of the process in motion at the same time.

A final caveat: Part 1 contains a lot of statements that will sound outlandish. Stuff like "The universe is your co-creative partner" or "The universe won't send you anything that is not in alignment with your authenticity." These statements will offend your rational mind. Your internal dialogue may sound something like "Where is she getting this stuff?!" or "What is she talking about?" or "Prove it!" I could have littered this book with citations of the work of scientists, physicists, thought leaders, and spiritual leaders who have explored these concepts and are trying to prove them with MRI brain scans and randomized controlled trials. But I'm not sure it would have helped assuage any skepticism.

Instead, these statements are the distillation of my twenty-year path from a life that felt like a beautiful prison to a life that feels peaceful, joyful, and aligned. In those twenty years, I read voraciously about health, wellness, and spirituality. I searched and searched for answers. I meditated. I followed the breadcrumbs and the synchronicities. As they say, the proof is in the pudding. But I had to make my own pudding. And you have to make your own pudding. The journey is yours. Books and philosophies and practices—this book included—can guide you along the way. But the truth is that all the answers lie inside you. As you read part 1, know that the name of the game is self-love and self-trust. Trust that if something feels resonant, it could be just the ingredient you need right now. And trust that if something feels dissonant or like total BS, you should feel free to disregard it. You're the sole expert.

Let's dive in.

CHAPTER 1

Uncover Your Authenticity

If financial planning is co-creating the life of your dreams, the first question is, What is the life of my dreams? The core concept here is authenticity. What is your core essence? What is important to you? What do you value? What is authentic to you? Authenticity seems like a deceptively simple concept, but it's important and relevant for two reasons.

First, the universe is your co-creative partner in this endeavor of crafting your dream life. I don't have any rational scientific evidence for this statement, but if you've ever had an experience in your life that feels like nothing short of a miracle, you've probably felt the power of co-creation. Perhaps it was the day you met your partner, or the day you held your child in your arms for the first time. Maybe it was a job opportunity that came through at just the right moment, or the synchronistic kindness of a stranger that came at just the right time. Whether we know it or not, we are always in co-creation with the universe. And one important principle is that the universe won't send you anything that is not in alignment with your authenticity. You can hope and pray for a dream job making millions on Wall Street, but if your soul is craving a career in entertainment, that Wall Street job is unlikely to come through or to stick, no matter how hard you try, how many times you try, how many credentials you get, or how much networking you do. Authenticity is important because it will be very difficult, if not impossible, to realize a dream that is not truly authentic to you.

The second reason authenticity is important is that it serves as a compass. In chapter 2, we'll talk about clearing our subconscious limiting beliefs, which can be especially insidious because they are, well, subconscious. We pick them up almost from the ether starting the day we're born. They might lead us to think that we want a big house, a fancy car, and a private jet. Or they might lead us to believe that we want a tiny house, a moped, and the life of a homebody. It's not that one set of desires is better than the other. It's that we get off course when there is misalignment between what we think we *should* want and what our soul authentically desires. Inner work is often described as peeling away the onion layers. And when it comes to authenticity and co-creating the life of your dreams, the work is to peel away all the things you think you "should" want in order to find what it is that you really want. For some lucky souls, authenticity comes easily. They are living, and have always lived, in pretty close alignment with their truth. For others of us, the road home to authenticity is a bit rockier. But in order to co-create the life of our dreams, we always have to point our compass to our true north star—our true authenticity.

For me, the road to authenticity was a bit winding. I grew up in a lovely suburb and was born to two loving, stable parents. I went to great schools, got married at twenty-three, and graduated from law school. Around age twenty-nine, I started to struggle. On the outside, everything was perfect. My husband and I lived in a beautifully appointed glass-box condo in downtown Chicago. He had cofounded a thriving healthcare start-up, and I was working for one of the world's largest international law firms. We were young and healthy, but I was crumbling on the inside. Everything felt increasingly heavy, like there was an unrelenting weight on my shoulders. Things that should have been joyous felt hard. And after eighteen months of heaviness, I, in a moment of desperation, pulled out a piece of paper. I started scribbling down everything I wanted in my life. It read something like "I want to get a dog. I want to move to a tiny house in Colorado. I want simplicity. I want to spend time in nature."

Uh-oh.

Over the course of the next three years, my entire life blew up. I got a dog. I moved to Wyoming. I went backpacking in the national parks. I switched careers from international tax law to financial planning. My husband divorced me. And on it went. Today, almost ten years later, I live in a log cabin in the woods. I married a guy who lives to be outside. We have a beautiful son and a simple life. I am obsessed with financial planning. And that sweet little doggy has been by my side through it all.

I firmly believe that financial planning has to start with your authenticity. Your true, deep authenticity. Money is wonderful, and it makes so many things in our life possible. And in order to attract more of it, it's important to think about what we want that money to do for us. If money were no object at all—if you had more money than you could ever possibly spend—what would life look like? How would you spend your time? Where would you live? Who would you spend time with? What would you contribute? And most importantly, how would you *feel*? If we don't spend some time contemplating the future we want and feeling into that future, it's entirely possible that we'll end up someplace we don't want to be. I don't want you to get far down the road of life only to find that, although you've had a successful career, earned and saved a lot of money, and achieved financial stability, you hardly recognize yourself or your life.

So how do we start peeling back the onion layers on our authenticity?

One approach is to grab a piece of paper and start freewriting, just like I did in one of my lowest moments. (I still do this periodically when I'm feeling adrift or off track.) Here are a few guidelines to get you started:

1. Turn off your brain. Freewriting isn't about getting conscious, coherent thoughts on a page. It's about letting words, ideas, and feelings flow through you.
2. It can be helpful to freewrite first thing in the morning, before you're fully awake. You can even keep your eyes half closed with a soft focus on the paper.
3. If no words are coming, feel free to just doodle or move the pen across the page while you wait for inspiration.
4. Don't censor yourself or limit yourself to certain topics. Feel free to write down anything that comes—random words, desires, ideas, dreams, challenges, fears, thoughts, feelings, etc.—without worrying about whether they're relevant or "correct."
5. Take as much or as little time as you need; there are no rules.

When you feel like you're emptied out, stop and reflect on

what has come through. I like to make a list of the most salient points, insights, and takeaways from my free writes.

Another approach is to use structured journaling. If you are feeling stuck or simply want some prompts to get you started, you can check out the Authenticity Journal Exercise in the appendix.

Another piece of the puzzle is that envy and jealousy are, counterintuitively, helpful tools in this process. Envy and jealousy are by no means emotions that we strive to feel in our day-to-day lives. But when they do arise, they can provide helpful hints to what our soul really wants. When you're hit with that lightning bolt of emotion, dig a little bit to understand what exactly it is that strikes you about that person or situation. It may be that it's something you're calling in for your own life.

Finally, Human Design is a system that has helped me. Human Design is an esoteric combination of astrology, the Chinese I Ching, Judaic Kabbalah, Vedic philosophy, and modern physics. The internet is full of mixed reviews and descriptions of Human Design. There are also a lot of Human Design apps and websites that you can reference. I find these online resources to be a bit confusing and conflicting, but I have really enjoyed customized one-on-one sessions with a Human Design reader. If you feel called to make that investment in yourself, I do think that a qualified Human Design reader can help you understand how you're wired. It can be validating to have another human tell you about how you best make decisions, how you best manage your energy, how you can tap into your intuition, and more. This is probably stuff you know deep down, but a little external mirroring can strengthen your self-trust and resolve. Again, take it for what it's worth, and explore it if, and only if, you feel called.

Your authenticity likely will evolve year over year and with different phases of your life. It can be helpful to check in with your authenticity periodically, and it can feel especially grounding to do some authenticity writing after a major life event (e.g., marriage, divorce, the birth of a child, illness, geographic relocation, etc.).

Ultimately, you never want to be that person who has money and is miserable. The fastest path to misery is to live someone else's life—to be stuck in someone else's vision of what it means to be happy, fulfilled, abundant, and successful. So let's get ruthlessly honest about what's authentic to you. And let's keep peeling back the onion layers, time and time again. As scary as this process may be, and as much destruction as may ensue, I believe that every force in the universe is pushing you toward your authentic wholeness. As Oscar Wilde said, "Be yourself; everyone else is already taken."

CHAPTER 2

Transform Your Subconscious Limiting Beliefs

It is often said that you are the creator of your own destiny. That is a frustratingly simple platitude when you're in the day-to-day grind, waking up, going to work, and trying to balance a budget, manage your kids, keep your relationship together, and get a moderately healthy dinner on the table. So in order to take this principle from platitude to empowering reality, we have to reexamine everything that we know. If there's only one thing that you take away from part 1 of this book, it is that your subconscious mind creates your external reality. Or, to put it another way, your external reality reflects what is going on in your subconscious.

This principle is both empowering and terrifying. It's empowering because it gets us thinking: How do I change my subconscious? Is it possible to change my subconscious? How can I put this principle to work in my own life? And this principle is terrifying because it requires radical responsibility. If your external, material circumstances—your finances, your home, your career, your relationships—are not quite what you want them to be, then it's time to take responsibility for what's rolling around in your subconscious mind and your inner world.

How do I know? I learned the hard way.

Eighteen months after my divorce, I opened *The Wall Street Journal*. My ex-husband's company had gone public. For about $11 billion. Billion with a *B*. And I opened the financial statements, and there it was. He was one of the highest-paid executives, personally worth $250 million. And he wrote me a check for $1.5 million. It was a lovely sum, but he may as well have written "BETRAYAL" in the memo line. We had mediated our entire divorce agreement in two hours because I insisted on an amicable process. And, as I learned from the newspaper that day, he had lied to my face about the value of his company in that mediation. We had spent thirteen years together and were married for ten. We fell in love in the library when I was a sophomore in college and he was a second-year medical student. I followed his career around the country while he was building his company. I carried the mortgage in my name alone when his start-up didn't have any income and the bank wouldn't lend to him. I earned the stable paycheck so that he could take on the risk. I was kind and loving. I was also codependent, weak, and naive.

Around that same time, eighteen months postdivorce, I was dating a guy who was an expert manipulator. He had spent several decades leading a "spiritual" organization that I think could only be described as a cult. So he had all the psychological tricks in the book. I broke up with him and he came after me with shocking vitriol. And it *finally* hit me like a ton of bricks: *"I am the common denominator."*

Uh-oh.

A few weeks after this betrayal-breakup shock wave, I was

contemplating my situation. And out of nowhere, it hit me. There was a program I had heard about on a podcast years prior called To Be Magnetic (TBM) by a woman named Lacy Phillips. It was a program that promised to help you manifest anything you truly desired in your life. Sign me up! I started TBM work that day. I did their thirty-minute guided meditations every day. Although the meditations come in different flavors and can help you work through a whole host of issues, I focused specifically on codependency, boundaries, and lack of personal strength, all of which were clearly issues for me. And nine months after starting these TBM meditations, I met the man of my dreams. We were married a year later.

To be fair, I also leaned hard on other co-creation tactics in those nine months leading up to our meeting. In terms of authenticity (chapter 1), I had to radically rethink the profile of the man I was "supposed" to marry. If I hadn't gotten really clear on what my soul truly desired, I probably would have missed my husband completely when he walked into that fateful dinner party. But because I had a clear picture of what was truly aligned, it felt like a lightning bolt when he walked into the room. I knew instantly that this was the man of my dreams. In terms of taking action (chapter 3), I had to get dressed and go to that dinner party. I had to listen to that little voice inside that told me to get up and go, even though I would have much rather stayed on my couch and cooked dinner at home. And in terms of clearing space (chapter 4), I had to pass tests. I had to break off a dead-end relationship with an unavailable man. I had to block and ignore a dangerously persistent ex-boyfriend. So it is true that subconscious reprogramming alone didn't bring me the man of my dreams. I had to have all the pieces in motion. But the subconscious work was certainly a core contributor to a successful co-creative process. I had to own my ugly truths and my shadow before the universe would deliver, which is a totally fair deal.

You're thinking, "Great story, but what does any of this have to do with money?"

I offer this narrative to illustrate our core principle: Your external reality is a reflection of your subconscious mind. And if you clear your subconscious limiting beliefs, you can start to craft a life that exceeds your wildest dreams. When we're faced with a problem on the material plane, whether it's in love, money, career, home, or otherwise, we often feel inclined to tackle it head on. You're spending too much money, so you download an app that helps you budget. You were denied a raise at work, so you take a class on how to negotiate for a higher salary. And sometimes those tactics do the trick—problem solved. But when the problem seems particularly stubborn or intractable, and you're feeling stuck and hopeless, and you're repeating the same patterns in your life again and again despite your best efforts, it's time to dig into the subconscious.

What are some examples of how this might play out in the realm of finance and career?

Let's say you were born into this world to be a musician. Both your parents are corporate lawyers. As a young child, your subconscious imprints that music is wonderful but that it's impossible to earn a living making music. Or you might imprint that in order to be loved, respected, admired, and safe in the world, you need to be a lawyer or a corporate type, not a musician. And the most insidious part of this programming is that even if your parents say verbally that they encourage your music career, even if they support you with lessons and instruments, and even if they genuinely believe you can succeed and want to see you succeed as a career musician, the modeling you observe can still trump the conscious, external words and actions of your parents.[1] Fast-forward many years.

---

1.   To be clear, this is in no way about blaming your parents or yourself or your life circumstances. No one is at fault, and no one is to blame—not you, not your parents, not the universe. We're simply acknowledging

You're a grown adult trying to build a professional music career. You find yourself stymied and floundering at every turn. You could work harder, push through, pull all-nighters, and hire a new agent. But it also could be transformative to get down into your subconscious and start to reprogram your neural pathways from "I have to be a corporate lawyer to be loved, respected, secure, etc." to "It is safe to be a professional musician." (More on neural reprograming techniques at the end of this chapter.)

To give another example, perhaps you grew up the daughter of first-generation US immigrants. Your parents never made much money but always encouraged you to do well in school, and they worked hard to save money for your college education. They always told you they wanted you to have more career opportunities than they had. Nevertheless, despite your parents' support and words of encouragement, you subconsciously imprinted that immigrants from your home country could only ever make $X per year or work in X kind of career. Today, you find yourself being turned down for promotions at work and unable to make the money you want to make. Subconscious reprogramming could help move the needle.[2]

In short, if your financial situation is in any way not what you want it to be, you likely have subconscious money blocks. Maybe you want to make more money. Maybe you want secure housing. Maybe you want to escape corporate life and start your own business or freelance gig or show. Maybe you want

---

that our brains are plastic and that certain neural pathways are laid down, especially in childhood when our brains are particularly malleable. For more on how and why these early experiences shape us, check out Bessel van der Kolk's *The Body Keeps the Score*.

2. I want to be emphatic about something here. There is a lot of shadow in the world. Racism, inequality, greed, narcissism, sexism, and all the other isms are, unfortunately, alive and well. All this talk about neural reprogramming and radical responsibility is in no way designed to excuse or minimize this very real stuff that you may bump up against in your life. No one deserves to be treated poorly. Period.

to gain some financial independence and stop relying on your partner, your family, or your trust fund. Here are some examples of other subconscious limiting beliefs that could be standing between you and your dreams:

- "I am unimportant."
- "I am unlovable."
- "I am undeserving."
- "I am powerless."
- "I am trapped."
- "I am overwhelmed."
- "I can't trust my judgment."

Again, these low-self-worth beliefs are often imprinted in childhood, despite the (generally) good intentions and best efforts of our parents, caregivers, teachers, siblings, and friends.

Layer on familial and societal messaging around money, and it's no wonder that you keep procrastinating on getting your money in order. Familial and societal messaging can include statements like these:

- "Just get a safe corporate job and stay in it."
- "Entrepreneurship is risky and reckless."
- "Women never make as much money as men."
- "Rich people are greedy a-holes."
- "You need a man to provide for you financially, so marry well."
- "Money is for everyone else, but not for us."
- "Money is evil."
- "Money is sinful."
- "Even if you have money, you'll lose it all and end up poor."
- "Money destroys relationships and comes between people."

- "Investing is too risky; just put your money under the mattress."
- "Credit card debt is a necessity of life. You just can't live without overspending."
- "You'll never make a good living unless you work sixty hours per week in a high-rise office building."
- "You can't make any money because you are too busy raising your kids."
- "What you have to say doesn't matter. No one wants to buy your product, service, course, etc."
- "The financial and economic system is rigged."

THE STRATEGY AND TACTICS

Sometimes I feel like there isn't a healing modality that I haven't tried. When I was twenty-one, I developed a wicked eating disorder, and it plagued me for over a decade. And in the course of healing from that, I became a human guinea pig. From talk therapy and art therapy to cognitive behavioral therapy, every antidepressant medication under the sun, eye movement desensitization and reprocessing (EMDR), internal family systems therapy, kundalini yoga, Bikram yoga, herbs, functional medicine, blood tests, breath work, flower essences, astrology, Enneagram, crystal healing, colonics, past-life readings, shamanic readings, life coaching, and more—the list of things I've tried is long.

When it comes to reprogramming the subconscious mind, I have found guided meditations to be incredibly helpful. Of course, like any medicine, the meditation should be tailored to the particular issue you are looking to transform. But if you're looking for a place to start, I have found that the guided meditations from To Be Magnetic are incredibly effective. If you are coming to neural reprogramming with a high level of day-to-day stress or a history of trauma, it can be helpful to add some generalized meditation to your routine as well. The more relaxed you are, the easier it is to open the subconscious and rewire it. For this generalized level-setting and ground-work, my top favorites are Transcendental Meditations and/or an acupuncturist with an orientation toward spiritual healing. These modalities can be invaluable for clearing stress from the mind and body.

Specific recommendations aside, why do these things work? Or how do these things work? What's the mechanism? Whether it's meditation, yoga nidra, or acupuncture, these modalities allow you to access what Deepak Chopra calls the "field of pure potentiality."[3] This field goes by numerous names. You can call it the quantum field, the void, the blackness, the bliss field, the nothingness. But it is the field where all possi-bility resides. It is the field from which all creation emerges. Everything in physical form in our three-dimensional world is born from this field. I don't really know how to put words to it, other than to say that it is worth experiencing firsthand. Or if you've ever looked at a newborn baby and wondered, "Where did you *come* from?" (other than, of course, sperm, egg, and zygote), you've contemplated the field of pure potentiality.

When you spend time communing with the field of pure potentiality, miracles will catalyze in your life. Please don't ask me when, why, or how those miracles will catalyze. That is certainly above my pay grade, and those questions are not in the realm of human knowledge, determination, or control. It's not up to us. But trust that the more you let go of control and expectations and timelines, the more you sink into trust, and the more you commune with the field, the more those miracles will catalyze in time.

---

3.   Deepak Chopra, *The Seven Spiritual Laws of Success* (New World Library, 1994).

At the end of the day, if my divorce had gone differently, I would have been riding off into the sunset with tens of millions of dollars in the bank. But truth be told, I wouldn't change a thing. I learned so many valuable lessons from that experience, and first among them is that we are in constant, powerful co-creation with the universe. There are a million subconscious reasons we believe that we can't make money doing what we love. We believe we have to sacrifice our lives and our health and our relationships for work. We believe there's a trade-off between time and money. We believe resources are scarce. We believe we can't be both spiritual and rich. The garbage stories we're telling ourselves subconsciously are reflected in our checking account balance. When we use meditation to start to rewire our subconscious minds, the problems in our lives that once seemed intractable—financial, professional, relational—can magically transform. Although it's not your fault, the power is in your hands.

CHAPTER 3

Find Your Unique Contribution

So much ink has been spilled about "finding your purpose" in life. I think this phrasing misses the mark and puts way too much pressure on career. You are not defined by what you do or by how much you accomplish in a day. Your purpose is that you exist. Your purpose can be summed up in the phrase "I am." The fact that you are here, on this planet, in human form, at this time, is your purpose. So don't worry about finding your purpose.

As we explored in the introduction to part 1, we take the "yes and" approach to creating wealth and abundance. We do the inner work in order to connect with the vertical. And we do the outer work in the horizontal. This chapter is about the outer work—that horizontal. It's no secret that money and abundance come from work and career, and we certainly don't subscribe to the theory that you can repeat affirmations in the mirror every morning and watch money rain down on you from the heavens. But there is so much confusion about what *work* means. And many of us swing the pendulum too far in the other direction. We're not waiting for money to rain down on us. We are pushing, pushing, pushing. We are working fifty-plus hours a week. We're stuck in jobs we hate. We count the days to retirement. And we feel like we have to get out there and make things happen.

Is there a more balanced concept of work? What if we defined work as "service through joy" rather than "servitude through suffering"? This is an important compass. I don't think that work is the enemy. I think that each one of us wants to find expression for our life force. Each one of us wants to use our unique talents, gifts, and experiences to serve. When we ditch the concept of your "purpose," we are left with the concept of your *contribution*. There is a contribution to be made on this planet that you, and only you, can make.

How do I know that you have a unique contribution to make? I don't know. I'm not inside you. But my sense is that, in your quiet moments, there is a longing—something you want to bring to life. Maybe your professional and financial life is already dialed in. Maybe you are doing work you love through a vehicle you love and making all the money you ever need and want. Or maybe you're at the opposite end of the spectrum. Maybe you're stuck in a job you hate, have no idea what you want to contribute, and feel financially trapped. Or maybe you're somewhere in between. Perhaps you're in the right industry but the wrong vehicle and are seeking a better work environment and a bit of a raise. Maybe you're sixty-eight years old and building your first career. Maybe your calling is full-time parenthood, which is one of the most demanding careers there is.

Wherever you fall along the spectrum, there are a few core principles to apply here. We've already covered the first two principles: authenticity and clearing the subconscious.

The more you put these two principles to work—the more you excavate your authenticity and the more you clear your subconscious—the stronger your calling and creative force will become. And the easier it will be to move out of servitude through suffering and into service through joy. Again, as we talked about in the last chapter, it's no secret that the world can be hard on our authenticity and on our subconscious, especially when we are young and our brains are so plastic. Maybe your soul-level calling is in geology, but you were raised by two concert pianists, and so you imprinted that music was the only safe path. Or vice versa. Maybe you're called to be a pianist, but you imprinted that geology is the only safe path. No matter the details, authenticity will help you crystallize your soul-level calling and subconscious unblocking will help you feel, on a deep soul level, that you are safe to pursue that calling. The goal is alignment between authenticity, mind-heart, and action-contribution.

The third principle to add here is the principle of "creation, maintenance, and destruction." In Hinduism, there are three deities: Brahma the creator, Vishnu the preserver, and Shiva the destroyer. We can observe cycles of creation, maintenance, and destruction in nature, and we can observe them in our own lives. The idea here is that if you're not leading with creation, then destruction is nipping at your heels. We often believe that staying in a job we hate and collecting a paycheck is the safest option. But I tend to think it's the riskiest. If you're treading water at work, it can't last forever. It's safer to move forward than it is to stay still because if you don't make a move, the universe will make it for you. Maybe you'll be formally demoted at work. Maybe you'll be functionally demoted and moved to a department that is irrelevant and invisible. If you're self-employed, maybe your business's revenue will drop sharply or all your clients will disappear at once. Maybe you'll be fired. The universe isn't trying to punish you in these situations. It's simply trying to push you into a path that is more authentic and more aligned. The lesson is to lead with creation.

Now certainly, there's a balance here. I'm not advocating that you switch jobs every six months for the rest of your life. I'm not advocating that you walk into work, throw coffee in your boss's face, and quit your job today. I'm not advocating for sudden, dramatic career changes or financially devastating professional decisions. But there is a balance. Maybe you start to take classes at night in a field that interests you. Maybe you volunteer on the weekends to explore a new industry. Maybe you start saving some money so that you have an escape fund—money that you can use to start your own business or go back to school or take some time off to transition between jobs. Maybe you start looking for a new job in the same line of work but with a company that has a culture or mission that feels more authentic to you.

THE STRATEGY AND TACTICS

There are two threads to the question "What is my contribution?" The first is a question of subject matter. In other words, where do your interests lie? What do you like to read about? Think about? Are there industries or environments you feel drawn to? What are your favorite topics? The second thread is the question of heart. What kind of energy do you want to put into the world? What pulls at your heartstrings? What is your personal ethos? By looking at the overlap between your interests and your heartfelt desires, you can start to suss out the contribution that only you can make.

To take one example, maybe you've always been drawn to the subject matter of education. And from a heart perspective, you feel called to guide and mentor. The thought of teaching in a traditional big classroom setting feels overwhelming, chaotic, and unsatisfying. You yearn to help students follow their own unique passions and interests in a customized way, so perhaps you decide that bespoke one-on-one tutoring is your unique contribution. Or, to use another example, maybe you have a heartfelt vision of oneness and innovation that you want to put into the world. You feel called to lead and motivate a group of educators forging a new path, and so you become the founder and CEO of an international chain of charter schools.

There are two tools that can help you discern where your interests lie and what your heart feels called to express. The first is the Gene Keys personality testing system, and the second is journaling. Specifically, for journaling, I like to take out a piece of regular notebook paper and draw a line down the center. I title the left-hand column something like "All the things I want in job and career," and I title the right-hand column something like "All the things I don't want." And then I sit down and start writing my lists. Like with the Authenticity Journal Exercise in the appendix, this is for your eyes only. So don't feel like you have to filter or censor. Make your lists as long as you want. Don't worry about what you think you "should" want, and don't constrain yourself to what you think is possible or realistic. Dream big and write freely. You might not get everything on your wish list in the near term, but you might also be surprised at how much you do get.

Money and abundance come from work, but work shouldn't be misery. As sovereign, autonomous, divine beings, we all have a desire to serve, and we each have a unique contribution to make.

CHAPTER 4

Pass Tests and Clear Space

There is a fourth step in the co-creative process: Pass tests and clear space.

This principle is one of the key principles of money energetics. And because it's an energetic, the only way I can really describe this is by feel. So let's say you've been putting the first three principles into play consistently. You've been living in your authenticity. You've been meditating and doing your subconscious work. And you're contributing in that way that only you can. You're doing the work that you are designed to do. The universe is almost ready to send you something miraculous. But it wants to know: Are you really committed to growth? Are you really ready to ditch the old and live in the new?

Like we said in the introduction to part 1, the universe has your back. It wants you to experience peace and abundance and freedom. It wants you to overcome all those limiting beliefs that cloud the true nature of your essence—the fact that you are a whole, sovereign, divine being who is having a human experience. One of the rewards for growth is material success and financial abundance. But, like an infinitely patient parent, the universe will test you. Before it gives you the keys to the car, it will ask you to demonstrate your growth and your maturity. There are two ways to demonstrate your growth and maturity: passing tests and clearing space.

PASSING TESTS

Tests are exactly what they sound like. They are opportunities, situations, or feelings that tempt you back into an old way of being. They also test your faith and resolve. For example, let's say you've left your job and have started your own firm— something you've always dreamed of doing. You're two months into the new venture, you're getting traction, but you're certainly still in start-up mode. Then, a recruiter calls with a job offer. You'd be making a ton of money, but it would put you right back into a work culture and environment that you know isn't aligned. As scary as it is, you probably need to decline to interview for that job.

Of course, there are no hard-and-fast rules, and each situation is different. But it is important to be on the lookout for tests. The universe isn't trying to punish you or tempt you. It's simply giving you opportunities to grow and evolve. Another example: me and my relationship with the unavailable partner. It was a test. I had to break off that relationship and sever all contact with that person before the universe sent true love.

CLEARING SPACE

Physical Space

Physical space is about clutter. Is your home full of things you never use? That old pair of jeans that's two sizes too small? That broken pot that's beyond repair? Your six rolls of Scotch tape? Eight Phillips-head screwdrivers? It's time to clean out and donate, sell, or recycle. One day, I hope that we'll live in a world of closed-loop manufacturing and production, where every material thing can be kept in circulation. But until that day comes, do the best you can to find good homes for your old things. Accept that there may be some waste, and be discerning about what you add to your collection going forward.

Physical space can also include expenses that are not aligned. If you take inventory of your spending, for example, you might discover some extraneous expenses:

1. You are paying $6 per month for software you never use.
2. You are paying $90 per month because your ex-boyfriend is still on your cell phone plan.
3. You are paying $1,000 per month for a luxury car even though luxury isn't authentic to you and you would be happier driving a less expensive car.
4. You are spending $6,000 per year on personal flights even though you hate flying and would prefer road trips, camping, or regional getaways.

Clearing space might mean that you log in and cancel that software subscription. You call the cell phone company and remove your ex-partner from your account. You investigate whether you can break your car lease or sell your car. Or you adjust your routine so that you are not spending money on things, people, or services that aren't true to you.

Emotional Space

Emotional space is about discernment and boundaries. Discernment and boundaries are just as important as love and kindness. In fact, one cannot exist without the other. As good people who want to carry light into the world, we often give and give and give (e.g., me in my first marriage). We overextend ourselves and are left feeling exhausted, sick, and drained. In the extremes, we allow others to manipulate us and to take advantage of us, and we are left completely hollow. Discernment and boundaries are our friends; without them, there is no emotional space to receive what we need from the universe.

In the realm of emotional space, ask yourself what it is you'd like to say no to. Are there "friendships" in your life that leave you feeling drained? People who don't treat you well? A lover who takes and takes and takes? Social engagements that feel like burdens rather than celebrations? An abusive boss? Advertisements, media, or social media that make you feel less than or destroy your sense of peace and well-being? The word *no* is our best friend.

Mental Space

Mental space is about peace and sanity. What is causing you stress and anxiety? Do you have too many calendar appointments? Too many emails? Too many errands? Too many chores? What can you eliminate? What can you delegate?

Electronic clutter also takes up mental space. Do you have five thousand unread emails? A cloud drive full of receipts from ten years ago? Ninety apps on your phone? Can you delete? Can you unsubscribe?

At the end of the day, creation requires mental space. There's a reason that poets and songwriters retreat to beachside shacks and secluded studios. And there's a reason that you can't get any focused work done with constant interruptions from your boss and infinite meeting invitations from your coworkers.

Energetic Space

Energetic space is the realm of letting go. Here, we release control and we release expectations. This can be the hardest and most counterintuitive part of dancing with the universe. As humans, we want certainty. But here, it is imperative to embrace uncertainty, both with respect to the when and the what. We have to trust that the universe delivers what we need, when we need it.

About six months after my now-husband and I got married, I was in a psychedelic-assisted therapy session. About halfway through the session, I saw a bright-white light in my uterus. I sat up, ripped off my eye mask, looked right at my facilitator, and said, "I'm pregnant!" To which he responded gently, "Oh, that's wonderful! Why don't you lie back down and close your eyes?" At his instruction, I lay back down and got a crystal-clear seven-point download: (1) I'm pregnant, (2) this is going to be our only child, (3) I am not to use birth control, (4) my husband is not to get a vasectomy, (5) we are not to abort this baby, (6) the baby is going to be healthy, and (7) this baby is going to bring us more joy than we've ever known. Fortunately for the health of our child, I wasn't actually pregnant during the therapy session. But six weeks later, I was in fact pregnant. And the second I peed on that stick and saw those two blue lines, I knew instantly that this was the child

who had appeared to me six weeks earlier. And he is the ut-
most divine gift in every way and in every sense. My point is
that the universe gives you what you need, when you need it,
even if it wasn't part of your mind's five-year plan.

Impatience is also a natural phenomenon, especially when
we start meditating and co-creating. Maybe we've been meditating for three days, or three months, or even three years.
And then we start to ask, quite understandably, "Where's my
miracle? Why hasn't XYZ happened yet?" But as humans in
the co-creative partnership, we have to remember that there's
a division of labor. We follow our authenticity, clear our junk,
make our contributions, and clear space, and the universe
handles the details and, most importantly, the timing. If we
are mired in control, impatience, and anxiety, we don't leave
any energetic space for the universe to deliver. Trust and surrender not only help create energetic space, but they also facili-
tate good timing. Perhaps you can think back on a time in your
life when, in retrospect, everything unfolded serendipitously
at the perfect time and in the perfect way. Although it can be
hard to see when you're going through something, divine timing is often at play behind the scenes.

Conclusion

Clearing space should be easy, but sometimes it's deceptively
difficult. We have layers of conditioning that can work against
us. Maybe we hold on to those old objects because we subconsciously believe we're going to be poverty stricken. Maybe we
believe that if we decline a social invitation, we'll be forever
sad and alone. Maybe we're used to being overscheduled and
running all over town. Here, the principles of authenticity and
subconscious transformation can work in tandem with the
principle of clearing space. When you do the inner work, it can
be easier to say no and to clear space, even in the face of an

external world that demands a lot. And it can be easier to trust divine timing. At the end of the day, you have full permission to drop the things that you think you "should" want in favor of those things you authentically need.

CHAPTER 5

Co-Create the Life of Your Dreams—A Case Study

Co-creation becomes an upward spiral with dedicated practice. You build faith in the co-creative process as small changes and synchronicities appear in your life. Then, a major dream might come through, whether it's a big raise, a new job, paying off all your credit card debt, a new love relationship, or perhaps a new home. As you acclimate to your dream life and settle into your new level of reality, you also have an opportunity to deepen your authenticity.

As you engage in the process of realigning your life through co-creation, you might find it helpful to go back and revisit chapter 1. You might find that, as you peel back the onion layers on your childhood and societal programming, your true authenticity will come into sharper focus. This is not to say that the first version of your authenticity journaling will be so dramatically different from the version you write several years later. But it is to say that the later version of your authenticity could be even more crisp and clear. You simply might not tolerate things that you used to accept as inevitable or things that you used to do with resignation or out of obligation. As you set boundaries and cut out the things that you "should" or "could" or "maybe will" do, you have space to see in clear relief the things that really are your "heck yeses"—the things that light your soul's path.

In short, there is a positive reinforcing loop. The manifestations that appear in your life reflect your authenticity, and your newly co-created dream reality also gives you a platform from which you can continue to deepen and refine your authenticity, which in turn creates more energetic space for more goodness to come through.

In time (or perhaps today), you might find your soul craving "simplicity, stability, surrender, and stillness," as Carissa Schumacher describes in *The Freedom Transmissions*. Money can buy a lot of things, but it can also buy simplicity and stability. It can allow you to work less, to be present with your loved ones, to spend time in your garden, to take long walks in nature. It can alleviate the stress of an unexpected bill or housing insecurity. This simplicity and stability in turn can help you deepen your connection to spirit. Because, at the end of the day, this human experience is always a balance of two things at once. It is both material and spiritual. It is horizontal and vertical. It is doing and being. It is faith *and* discernment: dreaming big and executing with discipline and devotion.

A CASE STUDY

Let's look at an example to help bring these last four chapters together.

Take Abby. Abby does the authenticity exercise in the

appendix and discovers that she values (1) technology, (2) family, (3) travel, and (4) creativity. Abby is twenty-eight years old. Her parents divorced when she was sixteen; her mom was a successful fashion designer who ran her own firm, and her dad stayed home to raise Abby and her brother. After college, Abby moved to central Indiana to work as a marketing associate for a Fortune 500 company that makes cereal and other food products. She has been with her company for seven years, has found success, and recently got a promotion and a 15 percent raise. She feels okay about her financial position but dreams of starting her own marketing agency that caters to technology start-ups; feels frustrated that, no matter how hard she tries, she can't seem to save money for the down payment on a house; and is embarrassed that her 401(k) is sitting in cash because she hasn't had the courage to invest it.

Abby is growing increasingly depressed and is starting to dread going to work. Sunday evenings are the worst. She decides that the pain of staying put exceeds the pain of growth, so she starts doing some subconscious work. Abby gets down into her subconscious and quickly discovers that although her mom modeled that women can be extremely successful and powerful entrepreneurs, she subconsciously believes (rightly or wrongly) that her mom's career success was to blame for her parents' divorce. Abby subconsciously fears that if she starts her own firm, she'll never have the joyous family life that she craves. She also realizes that she is trying to save for a house because she thinks that's what you're "supposed" to do. She is good at saving money and has a healthy 401(k), but she can't seem to save for a house because homeownership just isn't aligned with her authenticity. Finally, Abby realizes that her dad was always talking about day-trading and investing and was always watching CNBC. He was self-conscious about not having income or a career of his own, and so Abby

subconsciously associates investing with shame and desperation. No wonder she hasn't invested her 401(k).

Abby decides to open a savings account for her future
marketing business. Her goal is to set aside one year of living expenses and a little for business start-up expenses so that
she can quit her job and open her agency without having to
borrow money or take on outside investors. Abby reduces her
401(k) contribution a little bit but finds joy in saving for her
goal of self-employment. It flows more easily than saving for a
house she never wanted. Abby also starts to read books on investing by younger female authors who don't remind her of her
dad, and she talks to peers and girlfriends about how they invest their 401(k)s. If they can do it, she can do it too. Out of the
blue, Abby's brother invites her on an all-expenses-paid ten-
day trip to Mexico that he won at a charity auction. The trip
is perfectly aligned not only with Abby's love of travel but also
with her desire for more family time. It's the universe's way
of saying "Keep going!" Finally, Abby stops spending so much
money on designer clothes and shoes. Abby realizes that her
purchases are a relic of her mother's love for fashion but not
a reflection of Abby's unique authenticity. It turns out Abby
doesn't want the latest and greatest handbag and would rather
have the latest technology, which her company just happens to
subsidize.

Fast-forward a year, and Abby is still doing her subconscious reprogramming work every day. She has also started
meditating and is finding flow. After years of dating all the
wrong people, Abby finally met the woman of her dreams—
Olivia—at a local pottery workshop. It was Abby's first major
manifestation. She also just topped off her savings account and
officially has enough money to start her marketing firm. Abby
is feeling like it's time to leave her job and move to California
to be closer to her parents, brother, and potential tech clients.

Abby's boss calls her into her office. Abby has been such a strong performer this last year that her company wants to give her a second promotion and raise. Abby feels the weight of this moment. This is the pivotal decision point. The universe is asking Abby, "Will you settle for something you don't really want, or are you going to follow your dreams?" After all, who turns down a promotion and raise at a stable company?! Abby goes back and redoes the authenticity exercise. There are elements of the new corporate role that do align with Abby's authenticity. The new role has a creative element. It has a big technology stipend. It offers paid time off and gives Abby and Olivia the time and budget to travel. It's a hard decision, but Abby knows, deep in her body, what she has to do. She's terrified, but she takes the leap of faith. Abby and Olivia pack the car and drive west to start their new life in California.

REFLECTIONS

If you've made it this far into this book, it's obvious that you're not someone who settles. You feel a strong pull to follow your soul's calling and purpose. You think differently, and you refuse to accept that your life must look a certain way just because you've been told that's "how things are." We applaud and celebrate your growth mindset. And we know there will be days where you wonder why on earth you do this co-creative dance, why you demand so much of life, and whether you should just give up and take the path of least resistance.

Money and money problems are so often framed as matters of personal discipline. Or as a world of spreadsheets, numbers, and trackers. But that belies the fact that money is just energy. The people who are making tons of money doing exactly what they want to do *and* who are investing in companies that similarly are doing impactful and significant things in the world don't just have more discipline and better spread-sheets. They have high subconscious self-worth.

The things that are going well in your life reflect areas where you have high subconscious self-worth and are living in alignment with your authenticity. If you are great at earning money but horrible at saving and investing, that's information. If you are great at earning money and great at saving but horrible at investing, that's information. If you are horrible at earning money but great at saving and investing, that's information. And if you are horrible at earning money and horrible at investing but you're good at saving, that's also information. Change your mind—your subconscious neural programming—and you can change your financial situation. You deserve to earn, spend, save, and invest well.

If neural reprogramming is such a big piece of the puzzle, why do we resist doing the work? The reality is that our brains and bodies necessarily circumscribe painful memories because our very core believes that we must compartmentalize the pain to survive. In order to get through the day and keep moving, it is more efficient for our bodies and our beings to simply shove the pain down, store it away, and move on. This automatic efficiency play works for our bodies and minds in the short term but holds us back in the long run. It's not surprising, then, that we resist "doing the work" until we are absolutely forced into it.

In fact, this is one way to make sense of the struggles and challenges we face in our lives. Financial, professional, personal, or relational challenges are not punishment from the universe. They are actually invitations. The universe sends you challenges because it wants you to grow, and it wants you to discover the light of your own sovereign divinity. If you view these pain points as a chance to grow, you start to dance with the universe and co-create the life of your dreams. If you interpret these pain points as punishment, believe that you are a victim of circumstance, or fall into despair and low self-esteem, you are missing the opportunity to do the inner work and co-create the life you truly want.

In short, I hope these chapters have inspired you to begin your co-creative practice and move closer not only to your financial goals but also to the life of your dreams.

PART 2

Bucketing

The second step of the financial planning process is to *bucket*.

Bucketing is a deceptively simple concept. It means that you have a unique bank account or "bucket" for each goal. You have a checking account for your routine spending. You might have an account to set aside taxes if you're self-employed. You might have an account to hold the savings for your upcoming dream vacation or kitchen remodel. And you'll likely want an account for long-term savings and wealth building, because everyone needs a nest egg. This long-term savings and wealth building is where we enter the realm of retirement accounts—complicated acronyms like *IRA* and strange tax code sections like 401(k)s and 403(b)s. Not to mention the alphabet soup of health-related accounts like HSAs and FSAs, and education savings accounts like 529s and Coverdell ESAs.

The concept of bucketing works because it triggers what academic experts call *mental accounting*.[1] Your brain exhales

---

1.   Richard H. Thaler and Cass R. Sunstein, *Nudge: Improving Decisions about Health, Wealth, and Happiness* (Yale University Press, 2021).

a big sigh of relief when it sees everything neatly organized and categorized. Better yet, bucketing has been shown time and again to increase the amount of money you save. It is essentially a mental trick that makes saving and spending feel reasonably effortless because it strikes the right balance between chaos and control in your financial life. You can spend more freely without having constant mental stress about whether you're meeting your financial goals.

So bucketing is easy and effective, and it holds incredible intuitive appeal. And we all want to be financially responsible—to feel organized, in control, and financially stress-free. But the reality is that the US legal and regulatory system is a morass. You go to get your accounts organized, and you face seemingly insurmountable questions and hurdles such as "Is a Roth IRA better than a traditional IRA?" and "Should I put money in an HSA or an FSA?" and "Can I contribute to a retirement account if I'm self-employed?" So you succumb to analysis paralysis. You, very reasonably, procrastinate. And then you feel bad that your financial life is out of control. Hear me when I say it's not your fault!

In part 2, we'll take a tour through the available account options and lay out the features and pros and cons of each type of account. My hope is that you will find confidence and peace of mind by bucketing your financial life. And my goal for part 2 is to give you the information you need to feel empowered to open accounts, close accounts, and implement an account structure that supports your unique goals and authenticity. There are no right or wrong answers. It's all about what works for you.

Let's dive in.

CHAPTER 6

Explore the Menu of Available Accounts

Checking accounts, savings accounts, money market accounts, brokerage accounts, retirement accounts—oh my! This chapter offers a glossary of different account types, many of which we discuss throughout part 2. Feel free to read it straight through or simply come back to it as a reference.

BANK

A bank is a company that is in the business of taking money from customers (called *depositors*) and loaning it out to other customers (called *borrowers*). Banks in the US need a charter to operate. A national bank is chartered by the Office of the Comptroller of the Currency, which is a federal agency inside the US Department of the Treasury. A state bank is chartered by a state banking authority.

CREDIT UNION

A credit union is a nonprofit organization. Like a bank, it takes money from depositors and loans it to borrowers. But credit unions must serve a discrete customer population in order to maintain nonprofit status. For example, credit union membership might be restricted to "people who live, work, or study in Washington State." Because credit unions are nonprofit, they typically can offer lower-interest-rate home or car loans to their members. National credit unions are chartered by the National Credit Union Administration, and state credit unions are chartered by a state authority.

BROKERAGE FIRM

A brokerage firm is a company that connects buyers and sellers. If you want to buy or sell investments like stocks, bonds, mutual funds, or exchange-traded funds (more on these in chapter 15), you will need a brokerage firm. Brokerage firms are generally registered with the US Securities and Exchange Commission (the SEC) and regulated by the Financial Industry Regulatory Authority (FINRA).

FINANCIAL INSTITUTION

A financial institution is an organization that deals with money, such as a bank, credit union, brokerage firm, or another type of financial company like an insurance firm, paycheck lender, or commodities dealer.

CHECKING ACCOUNT

A checking account is a product offered by banks and credit unions. You can deposit and withdraw money to handle your routine expenses, either by electronic transfer, with a paper check, or by using your debit/ATM card. You earn interest on the money inside your checking account, but it's generally pretty minimal.

HIGH-YIELD CHECKING ACCOUNT

A high-yield checking account is a checking account that pays a higher rate of interest than a normal checking account. But you have to read the fine print because high-yield checking accounts often impose a lot of tricky rules about how much you have to keep in the account, how many transactions you can execute per month, and whether the advertised interest rate will decrease over time.

SAVINGS ACCOUNT

A savings account is another product offered by banks and credit unions. The interest rate on a savings account is generally a touch higher than on a checking account. But some banks and credit unions say you cannot withdraw money from your savings account more than six times per month; if you do, they may charge a fee, close your savings account, or convert it to a checking account.

HIGH-YIELD SAVINGS ACCOUNT

A high-yield savings account is a savings account that pays a higher rate of interest than a normal savings account. But just like with a high-yield checking account, you have to read the fine print.

MONEY MARKET ACCOUNT

A money market account is a hybrid between a checking account and a savings account. It generally offers the slightly higher interest rates of a savings account but also allows you to write checks. At many institutions, a money market account is synonymous with a high-yield checking account. But details vary by institution, so always check the terms.

Money market accounts are also distinct from money market mutual funds. Money market mutual funds are an investment product (more on these in chapter 15), whereas money market accounts are a type of account.

BROKERAGE ACCOUNT (A.K.A. INVESTMENT ACCOUNT)

A brokerage account is a product offered by brokerage firms. You can buy and sell investments like stocks, bonds, options, mutual funds, and ETFs inside a brokerage account. Where checking, savings, and money market accounts only allow you to hold cash, brokerage accounts let you hold investments. A brokerage account is also called an *investment account*, and it is typically what you think of when you think of an investment account. That said, retirement accounts are also investment accounts because you can buy and sell investments inside a retirement account.

CASH MANAGEMENT ACCOUNT

A cash management account is a brokerage account that functions like a checking account. Many brokerage firms want to be a one-stop shop for their customers. But because brokerage firms are not chartered or regulated as banks, they cannot offer checking or savings accounts to customers. So cash management accounts look and feel like traditional checking accounts (e.g., no transaction limits, check writing, and an ATM/debit card) but invest your cash deposits in a money market mutual fund (i.e., an investment product) or ship your cash to a traditional bank every night.

RETIREMENT ACCOUNT

A retirement account is a tax-advantaged account that encourages people to save for retirement. Retirement accounts include things like traditional 401(k) accounts, Roth 401(k) accounts, traditional IRAs, and Roth IRA accounts. They also include traditional SIMPLE plans, Roth SIMPLE plans, traditional SEP plans, Roth SEP plans, 403(b) plans, 457(b) plans, and employee stock ownership plans.

401(K) PLAN

A 401(k) plan is a tax-advantaged retirement account that is set up and administered by a private company to help its employees save for retirement. Eligible employees can set up an account inside the company 401(k) plan and contribute part of their paycheck to that account.

Contributions to a traditional 401(k) plan are pretax contributions, which means that you get a deduction on your tax return in the year that you put money into your 401(k).

403(B) PLAN AND 457(B) PLAN

A 403(b) plan and a 457(b) plan are both very similar to a 401(k) plan. The difference is that while a 401(k) plan is set up and administered by a private company, a 403(b) plan generally is run by a nonprofit organization (e.g., school, church, hospital, charity, etc.) and a 457(b) plan generally is run by a governmental organization (e.g., state or local government).

SIMPLE 401(K) PLAN

SIMPLE stands for "Savings Incentive Match Plan for Employees." A SIMPLE 401(k) plan is a tax-advantaged retirement plan set up by a small business (i.e., a business with one hundred employees or fewer) for its employees. The small business either contributes a flat percentage of an employee's compensation to the employee's 401(k) account, or the business can match an employee's 401(k) contribution.

SOLO 401(K) PLAN

A solo 401(k) plan is a retirement account for solo entrepreneurs. Just like big companies can set up 401(k) plans, solo entrepreneurs can set up 401(k) plans only for themselves. Contrary to the name, a solo 401(k) plan can also cover your spouse if you work together in the same business.

SIMPLIFIED EMPLOYEE PENSION PLAN

A Simplified Employee Pension (SEP) plan is a tax-advantaged retirement plan set up by a company. Each eligible employee gets a SEP IRA under the plan, and the employer contributes to the SEP IRA to help fund the employee's retirement. Employees cannot contribute to a SEP plan. Self-employed people can set up their own SEP IRAs.

SARSEP

SARSEP stands for "Salary Reduction Simplified Employee Pension Plan." It is a SEP plan that was established before 1997. In 1996, Congress prohibited companies from setting up new SARSEPs. But SARSEPs that were established before 1997 are still around.

MONEY PURCHASE PLAN

A money purchase plan is a tax-deferred retirement account set up by an employer. Only employers are allowed to contribute money; employees cannot make contributions to a money purchase plan. But they can choose how to invest the money inside their accounts.

EMPLOYEE STOCK OWNERSHIP PLAN

An employee stock ownership plan (ESOP) is a tax-deferred plan that holds company stock. Companies will use ESOPs to give employees some ownership of the company in order to help incentivize employee performance. Employees cannot contribute to an ESOP or buy company shares inside the ESOP. Instead, the company funds the ESOP with cash or shares of company stock.

INDIVIDUAL RETIREMENT ACCOUNT

An individual retirement account (IRA) is a tax-advantaged account. An IRA is not tied to any particular employer, so you can set one up in minutes at any major brokerage firm in the US, regardless of whether you are employed or not.

SIMPLE IRA

Like a SIMPLE 401(k) plan, a SIMPLE IRA is a tax-advantaged retirement account set up by a small business (i.e., a business with 100 employees or less) for its employees. The small business either contributes a flat percentage of an employee's compensation to the employee's IRA, or the business can match an employee's IRA contribution. A self-employed person can also set up a SIMPLE IRA.

COVERDELL ESA

A Coverdell education savings account (ESA) is a special account designed to help pay for a child's education.

UTMA CUSTODIAL ACCOUNT

A Uniform Transfers to Minors Act (UTMA) account is an investment account that an adult manages for a child until the age of eighteen or twenty-one, after which time the money belongs to the child. The child can choose to spend the money on a college education—or blow it all on fast cars and designer shoes.

SECTION 529 PLAN

A Section 529 plan is a tax-advantaged account for education rather than retirement. Money in the account can be used to pay for K–12 education, college, graduate school, or certain federally designated apprenticeship programs. Section 529 plans are not tied to an employer; rather, they are run by the fifty individual US states and the District of Columbia, so fees and rules vary. Section 529 plans also come in two flavors: prepaid tuition plans and regular savings plans.

HEALTH SAVINGS ACCOUNT

A health savings account (HSA) is a tax-advantaged account for medical expenses, including health insurance deductibles and copays. Many employers offer HSAs and may contribute money to help employees put money aside for healthcare, but anyone with a high-deductible health plan can set up and contribute to an HSA, regardless of employment.

HEALTH FLEXIBLE SPENDING ARRANGEMENT

A health flexible spending arrangement (FSA), also known as a flexible spending account, is an account for certain out-of-pocket healthcare costs. FSAs are sponsored by employers and are not available if you are self-employed.

EMERGENCY SAVINGS ACCOUNT

In December 2022, Congress passed the SECURE 2.0 Act, which allows employers who sponsor retirement account plans to offer emergency savings accounts. Eligible employees can set aside part of their paycheck in an emergency savings account, and employers may match any funds that the employee contributes to help employees put aside a little money for emergencies.

DONOR-ADVISED FUND

A donor-advised fund (DAF) is a tax-advantaged investment account for charitable giving. If you would like to set aside money for charity but have yet to decide which charity you'd like to support, a DAF can be a good place to store the money. A DAF can also make sense if you are earmarking a lot of money for charity but don't want to donate the money to the charity all at once. That said, because a DAF adds an extra layer of complexity, it really only makes sense if you're giving tens of thousands of dollars to charity each year.

DAFs have become a popular alternative to private foundations. A private nonoperating foundation is a charitable organization that is funded by a small group of people—generally a single individual or a family—to grant money to other nonprofit organizations. (Big names in this space include the Ford Foundation and the Gates Foundation, along with tens of thousands of other smaller foundations.) Like a private foundation, a DAF allows a donor to grant money to other nonprofit organizations over time but without the administrative complexity (and associated cost) of a private foundation.

TRUST

A trust is not a particular type of bank account or investment account but rather is a separate legal entity. There are myriad different types of trusts—revocable trusts, irrevocable trusts, charitable trusts, and more. Trusts generally come into play when someone starts thinking about estate planning (i.e., "What will happen to my money and stuff when I die?"). Trusts can be a useful way to give money to someone but with some limitations and restrictions on how the money can be spent. They can also reduce or eliminate federal and state-level transfer taxes, including estate tax, gift tax, inheritance tax, and generation-skipping transfer tax.

CHAPTER 7

Customize Your Personal Account System

Many financial planning books extol the virtues of budgeting and tracking. We are told to download apps and save receipts. We monitor every penny. We track, control, and obsess. And then we feel guilt, shame, and fear when we are over budget one month or can never seem to stick to our spending plan. Worse yet, once we're over budget, the "eff it" mindset kicks in. "I've already blown it, so I may as well keep spending."

Bucketing can help break this cycle because it strikes a nice balance between control and chaos. It makes it easier to monitor our spending and our progress toward our financial goals without making us feel like we're white-knuckling a budget.

Over the course of these next chapters, we'll help you take control of your account structure. You might find that you need to open new accounts. For example, you might switch from a traditional checking account to a high-yield checking account.

You might also find that you need to consolidate some of your existing accounts. For example, if you have three checking accounts, you can consider closing two of them. If you have a 401(k) with an old employer, you can consider rolling that money into an IRA. Finally, if you have old, dormant, or empty accounts, consider closing them so that there is one less vector of attack for identity thieves or cybersecurity breaches.[1]

Let's dive in.

Big picture, there are three categories to consider. Category one is for your routine inflows and outflows. For many people, this is the checking account where you deposit your paycheck and pay your credit card bill. If you're a business owner or are self-employed, category one might also include a business checking account in the name of your legal entity (e.g., an LLC, corporation, etc.). And if you're self-employed or have a lot of investment income, category one might include a tax-reserve account where you set aside money to cover upcoming tax bills (more on tax reserves soon). Category two encompasses midrange and long-range financial goals. For many people, this includes saving for a home, retirement, or college. It can also include things like travel, home renovations, upcoming medical expenses, parental leave, etc. Category three encompasses moon-shot goals. These often include starting your own business, investing in private companies or start-up companies, giving to charity, and leaving money to children or heirs when you pass away.

---

1.   One caveat to the "close your account" concept: It doesn't necessarily apply to credit cards or lines of credit. Your FICO credit score is based in part on the ratio of available credit to the credit that you are actively using. Strangely, your credit score improves if you have a lot of credit available but are only using a small percentage of it. For this reason, it can be good to cut up and throw away old credit cards but keep the line of credit open. If you do close an account, make sure you download account statements and tax forms before you close it, as some institutions remove your online account access if you no longer have active accounts with their company.

I lay out these three categories solely to help us structure our thinking. This is in no way to imply that home buying or philanthropy are things that you "should" be aiming for. Again, it's all about what's authentic to you. This also in no way implies a hierarchy. For example, just because philanthropy is in category three, it doesn't mean that you can't give money to charity while you're saving for a down payment on your first home. Or that you can't be an angel investor while also saving for a child's college education. It is absolutely appropriate to allocate money toward more than one financial goal at a time, regardless of which category the goal falls into. Finally, from a bucketing perspective, you might find that you need more than one unique account in a particular category. For example, you might find that a personal checking account is all you need inside category one, but that you need a retirement account and a health savings account to cover category two. Or that you need both a personal checking account and a business checking account to cover category one but that you only need a retirement account inside category two.

Let's look at each category in more detail.

CATEGORY ONE

Routine Spending

You likely already have a checking account to manage your routine inflows and outflows. Checking accounts are pretty generic, and most have low fees. Yield is the biggest consideration. Standard checking accounts pay very little interest. High-yield checking accounts pay interest that is closer to the prevailing US federal funds rate. A quick search for "federal funds rate today" will show you that interest rate, and it can be helpful to look for a checking account that pays something approximating that annual interest rate. Even if a checking account isn't explicitly labeled *high yield*, the bank may be offering a favorable interest rate. Money market accounts and cash management accounts can be nice alternatives to traditional checking accounts and high-yield checking accounts because both account types generally pay nice rates of interest. Bottom line: Even the money inside your checking / money market / cash management account should be working for you, so make sure your account, whether personal or business, has low fees and high yields.

If you want to take your savings to the next level, consider keeping your checking account(s) at one financial institution and your mid- and long-range accounts at a different financial institution (or institutions). Some studies have shown that this segregation between your checking account and your goal-oriented accounts can help boost your savings percentage with very little conscious thought required on your part.

Tax Reserves

Income and property taxes can sneak up on you. If you are an employee who receives an Internal Revenue Service (IRS) Form W-2 from your employer every year, then you might not need a tax account. This is because your employer already withholds part of your paycheck and sends that part of your salary to the IRS every quarter. However, if you are self-employed, have a side hustle, own real estate, or have investments in a brokerage account, you'll likely need a place to park tax money because there is no automatic withholding on these types of income streams. You essentially act as your own employer, and you are responsible for sending money to the IRS every quarter.

Similarly, if you have a mortgage, it will often include a property tax escrow. Your bank will collect not only principal and interest for your mortgage every month but also money to cover your annual property taxes. Your bank will then send that property tax money to your town or county every year. However, if you don't have a mortgage or if your mortgage does not include an escrow, you will want to deposit money into a tax account periodically. There is nothing worse than getting a big annual tax bill and not having the cash to pay it.

You can park your tax-reserve money in a high-yield checking account or a high-yield checking account alternative (i.e., a money market account or cash management account). Like for your checking account, you want low fees and high yields. You can also stash your tax-reserve money in a high-yield savings account. The third option for your tax reserve is a brokerage account, also known as an investment account. Once the money is inside the brokerage account, you can invest it in CDs, Treasury bills, or a money market mutual fund. We'll talk more about these so-called cash-equivalent investment options in part 3. If you choose to go the brokerage-and-investment route for your tax-reserve money, you might get a slightly higher yield than you would on a high-yield checking account. But in most normal interest rate environments, the additional yield that you get by investing tax-reserve money inside a brokerage account won't be significant, so the simplest approach is likely a high-yield checking account, money market account, or cash management account.

CATEGORY TWO

There are many big purchases that can enrich our lives for years to come. There are tangible goods—furniture, fine jewelry, cars, boats, etc. There are intangible things like taking a big vacation, traveling the world, or taking time off to raise your kids, care for an aging parent, recover from illness or addiction, do spiritual work, go back to school, etc. Maybe you want to plan a big wedding. Maybe you're saving for a home, a vacation home, or a child's college education. Finally, there's retirement savings.

This is where we enter the world of tax-advantaged accounts. *Tax-advantaged account* is an umbrella term for different types of specialized savings accounts. The US Congress wants to incentivize people to save for things like retirement, college education, healthcare, and charitable giving. So it has established specialized savings accounts like 401(k)s, HSAs, and 529 college-savings plans. If you are saving for one of these financial goals, you can save a lot of money on your federal income tax bill in both the short and long term by opening a tax-advantaged account and housing your savings there.

Of course, tax-advantaged accounts do come with downsides. There are complicated rules about how much you can contribute. The investment options inside tax-advantaged accounts are sometimes limited. And you generally must use the money inside the tax-advantaged account for its intended purpose; if you don't, you might pay an income tax penalty. All these parameters vary depending on which type of tax-advantaged account is at play. For example, the rules for a traditional IRA are different from the rules for a Roth IRA. And we'll explore these contribution, investment, and distribution rules in greater detail. But the takeaway is that, in most cases, tax-advantaged savings accounts are worth a close look because the powerful tax benefits generally outweigh the complexity of their associated rules and restrictions.

The alternative to a tax-advantaged investment account is a brokerage account, which is a standard investment account. Brokerage accounts are often called *taxable accounts* because they don't carry any special tax benefits. Brokerage accounts also have a wide variety of investment options, unlike tax-advantaged accounts, which sometimes have limited investment options. But again, despite the headache, tax-advantaged accounts can significantly reduce the amount of federal income tax that you owe.

Let's take a closer look at the federal income tax benefits of tax-advantaged accounts. From a tax perspective, there are three things to think about with a tax-advantaged account: (1) Do I get a tax deduction when I contribute to the account (i.e., when I deposit money into the account, say, every year); (2) if I make an investment inside the tax-advantaged account and I earn money on that investment, do I pay tax on those profits; and (3) do I pay tax when I take a distribution from the account (i.e., when I withdraw money from the account)?

Do I get a tax deduction when I contribute to the account?

Income tax deductions are hardly intuitive. But a good way to understand them is to look at a copy of an income tax return (i.e., IRS Form 1040). Page 1 of the Form 1040 from 2021 first asks you to report every dollar that came in during the given calendar year. The definition of income is extremely inclusive. Income is not only your salary or your business income but also passive investment income like dividends, interest, and capital gains. It also includes prizes, alimony, certain social security income, jury duty pay, and so much more.

Form **1040** Department of the Treasury—Internal Revenue Service **U.S. Individual Income Tax Return**	**2024**	OMB No. 1545-0074	IRS Use Only—Do not write or staple in this space.

For the year Jan. 1–Dec. 31, 2024, or other tax year beginning _____ , 2024, ending _____ , 20 _____ See separate instructions.

Your first name and middle initial	Last name	Your social security number

If joint return, spouse's first name and middle initial	Last name	Spouse's social security number

Home address (number and street). If you have a P.O. box, see instructions.		Apt. no.	**Presidential Election Campaign** Check here if you, or your spouse if filing jointly, want $3 to go to this fund. Checking a box below will not change your tax or refund.
City, town, or post office. If you have a foreign address, also complete spaces below.	State	ZIP code	
Foreign country name	Foreign province/state/county	Foreign postal code	☐ You ☐ Spouse

Filing Status Check only one box.
- ☐ Single
- ☐ Married filing jointly (even if only one had income)
- ☐ Married filing separately (MFS)
- ☐ Head of household (HOH)
- ☐ Qualifying surviving spouse (QSS)

If you checked the MFS box, enter the name of your spouse. If you checked the HOH or QSS box, enter the child's name if the qualifying person is a child but not your dependent: _____

☐ If treating a nonresident alien or dual-status alien spouse as a U.S. resident for the entire tax year, check the box and enter their name (see instructions and attach statement if required): _____

Digital Assets At any time during 2024, did you: (a) receive (as a reward, award, or payment for property or services); or (b) sell, exchange, or otherwise dispose of a digital asset (or a financial interest in a digital asset)? (See instructions.) ☐ Yes ☐ No

Standard Deduction Someone can claim: ☐ You as a dependent ☐ Your spouse as a dependent
☐ Spouse itemizes on a separate return or you were a dual-status alien

Age/Blindness You: ☐ Were born before January 2, 1960 ☐ Are blind Spouse: ☐ Was born before January 2, 1960 ☐ Is blind

Dependents (see instructions):
If more than four dependents, see instructions and check here . . ☐

(1) First name　Last name	(2) Social security number	(3) Relationship to you	(4) Check the box if qualifies for (see instructions): Child tax credit	Credit for other dependents
			☐	☐
			☐	☐
			☐	☐
			☐	☐

Income

Attach Form(s) W-2 here. Also attach Forms W-2G and 1099-R if tax was withheld.

If you did not get a Form W-2, see instructions.

1a	Total amount from Form(s) W-2, box 1 (see instructions)	1a
b	Household employee wages not reported on Form(s) W-2	1b
c	Tip income not reported on line 1a (see instructions)	1c
d	Medicaid waiver payments not reported on Form(s) W-2 (see instructions)	1d
e	Taxable dependent care benefits from Form 2441, line 26	1e
f	Employer-provided adoption benefits from Form 8839, line 29	1f
g	Wages from Form 8919, line 6	1g
h	Other earned income (see instructions)	1h
i	Nontaxable combat pay election (see instructions) . . . 1i	
z	Add lines 1a through 1h	1z

Attach Sch. B if required.

2a	Tax-exempt interest . . .	2a	b	Taxable interest	2b
3a	Qualified dividends . . .	3a	b	Ordinary dividends	3b
4a	IRA distributions . . .	4a	b	Taxable amount	4b
5a	Pensions and annuities . .	5a	b	Taxable amount .	5b
6a	Social security benefits . .	6a	b	Taxable amount .	6b
c	If you elect to use the lump-sum election method, check here (see instructions) . . . . ☐				
7	Capital gain or (loss). Attach Schedule D if required. If not required, check here . . . ☐				7
8	Additional income from Schedule 1, line 10				8
9	Add lines 1z, 2b, 3b, 4b, 5b, 6b, 7, and 8. This is your **total income**				9
10	Adjustments to income from Schedule 1, line 26				10
11	Subtract line 10 from line 9. This is your **adjusted gross income**				11
12	Standard deduction or itemized deductions (from Schedule A)				12
13	Qualified business income deduction from Form 8995 or Form 8995-A				13
14	Add lines 12 and 13				14
15	Subtract line 14 from line 11. If zero or less, enter -0-. This is your **taxable income**				15

Standard Deduction for—
- Single or Married filing separately, $14,600
- Married filing jointly or Qualifying surviving spouse, $29,200
- Head of household, $21,900
- If you checked any box under Standard Deduction, see instructions.

For Disclosure, Privacy Act, and Paperwork Reduction Act Notice, see separate instructions. Cat. No. 11320B Form **1040** (2024)

From there, you get to take all your above-the-line deductions. This is anything above line 11 on Form 1040—adjusted gross income, or AGI. For example, let's say you had $60,000 come in the door in 2021 (i.e., you had $60,000 of gross income). Then, you look at Form 1040 Schedule 1 to see which above-the-line deductions you can take. Let's say you only have one above-the-line deduction—$3,000 for the traditional IRA contribution that you made in 2021. This means that in

2021, your adjusted gross income is $57,000. All else being equal, you'd rather pay federal income tax on $57,000 than on $60,000, so tax deductions are great.

However, not all tax-advantaged accounts generate a tax deduction when you contribute money. For example, you don't get a tax deduction when you put money into a Roth-style retirement account. That's why you'll often hear Roth-style accounts referred to as *after-tax* or *post-tax* accounts. In contrast, you generally do get a tax deduction when you put money into a traditional-style retirement account, which is why traditional-style accounts are often called *pretax* accounts.

If I make an investment inside the tax-advantaged account and I earn money on that investment, do I pay tax on those profits while they are in the account?

Tax-advantaged accounts are often called *tax-deferred* accounts. Or, you'll hear people say that money inside a tax-advantaged account "grows tax deferred." Tax deferral means that money you earn inside the account is not taxed as long as those earnings remain inside the tax-advantaged account. For example, let's say you contribute $1,000 to a Roth IRA this year. You invest that $1,000 in stocks and bonds. You earn $50 of interest this year on your bonds and you earn $50 of dividends this year on your stocks. You would normally have to pay federal income tax on that $100 of dividends and interest (i.e., your investment income). This means you might pay, say, $20 of tax on your $100 of investment income if your effective federal income tax rate is 20 percent. But because you bought the stocks and bonds inside a Roth IRA, which is tax deferred, you don't pay any tax on the $100. This is why tax-advantaged accounts are the darling of the financial planning industry. They really can save you a lot of money in taxes.

The other relevant concept behind tax deferral is the

capital gains tax. *Capital gain* is an income tax term. It is what happens when you sell almost any type of investment property, like stock, real estate, or even your home. For example, let's say you buy one hundred shares of Taiwan Semiconductor Manufacturing (TSM) stock for $50 per share in 2019. Your total cost basis in TSM stock is $5,000 (i.e., one hundred shares times $50 per share). In 2023, let's say TSM stock is trading for $110 per share. You sell your TSM stock for $11,000, which means you have a $6,000 capital gain (i.e., you made $6,000 on your investment). Ordinarily, that $6,000 of profit would be taxable income for federal income tax purposes. But if you bought and sold your TSM stock inside a tax-advantaged account, then your $6,000 of profit is not taxed when you sell your TSM stock.

Bottom line: Tax-advantaged accounts are incredibly powerful because you can earn investment income such as dividends, interest, and capital gains inside the tax-advantaged account and not pay federal income tax on those earnings when they hit the account. All tax-advantaged accounts are also tax deferred.

Do I pay tax when I take a distribution from the account?

There are two types of distributions from a tax-advantaged account: qualified distributions and nonqualified distributions. Qualified distributions are the types of distributions you'd expect. When you take money out of a retirement account at retirement age, that's generally a qualified distribution. Or, when you take money out of a health savings account to pay for medical expenses, that's a qualified distribution. When you take money out of a retirement account or health savings account at age twenty-five to pay for a tropical beach vacation, that's generally a nonqualified distribution because you're not using the money in the tax-advantaged account for its intended purpose.

Qualified or "normal" distributions may or may not be subject to federal income tax, depending on the type of account. For example, you will pay tax when you pull money out of a traditional IRA to spend in retirement because that is how the tax rules are written. The trade-off with a traditional IRA is that you get a tax deduction when you contribute money, but then you pay tax when you withdraw money for retirement. In contrast, the rules for a Roth IRA say that you don't get a tax deduction up front when you contribute money, but you do get to withdraw money tax-free to fund retirement. So qualified distributions may or may not be taxed, just depending on the tax rules for the particular type of tax-advantaged account you've chosen.

When it comes to nonqualified distributions, you may face not only taxes but also tax penalties. For example, with an HSA, you can withdraw money from the HSA at any age to pay for medical expenses (these withdrawals are tax-free), or you can wait until age sixty-five and withdraw money from the HSA for any reason, medical or nonmedical. You will pay regular income tax on money that you withdraw after age sixty-five if you do not use it for medical purposes, but there is no tax penalty. So let's say your regular federal income tax rate is 30 percent and the tax penalty rate is 20 percent. If you withdraw $1,000 from your HSA at age sixty-six to pay for a tropical beach vacation (a nonmedical expense), then you would pay $300 of tax on that $1,000 withdrawal. If you withdraw that same $1,000 for vacation at age sixty-four, then you would pay not only $300 of tax but also $200 of tax penalty on that $1,000 withdrawal.

As you think about pulling money out of a tax-advantaged account, the first question to ask is whether you are using the money for its intended purpose at the intended time (e.g., after retirement age). If you are, there may or may not be ordinary income tax. If you are not using the money for its intended purpose, then you need to think not only about whether there is ordinary income tax but also about whether there is a tax penalty. The rules about taxes and penalties on qualified and nonqualified distributions vary depending on which flavor of tax-advantaged account you're using.

CATEGORY THREE

Category-three goals—entrepreneurship, private company investing, philanthropy, and legacy building—take us into the world of legal entities, private equity funds, donor-advised funds, and trusts. Though these are important topics, they are generally beyond the scope of this book.

Bottom line: You can house your investments inside a normal taxable brokerage account. Or you can house your investments in a tax-advantaged account. Tax-advantaged accounts can help you make more money in the long run because you're generally paying less in taxes and keeping more money in your pocket. As long as you're willing to navigate the rules and restrictions of a tax-advantaged account, they can be a tax-savvy option.

In each of the chapters that follow, we'll do a deeper dive on specific flavors of tax-advantaged accounts: retirement accounts, education accounts, and health accounts.

CHAPTER 8

Use Retirement Accounts to Build Your Nest Egg

Retirement may not be your idea of a good time. You might want to "retire" at age thirty-five and have complete financial freedom. You might want to work until the day you die. Regardless of your feelings about retirement, retirement accounts are a big part of the personal financial planning landscape in the US.

Retirement accounts are also wildly confusing. It's difficult enough to figure out the rules for one type of account—who, what, when, where, why, and how you can contribute and distribute money. You then have the comparison-shopping exercise. Is Roth better than traditional? Should I use a 401(k) or an IRA? Is a defined benefit plan better than a defined contribution plan? Finally, you have the interactions among the different types of accounts. If I have a 403(b) plan at work, can I also contribute to my IRA? *Should* I also contribute to my

IRA? What happens if I contribute too much in a particular year?

We could walk through all the rules for each type of account, or even put those rules in an at-a-glance chart. But that doesn't necessarily answer the question that is probably of most interest: "What should I *do*?" So, in this chapter, we'll highlight some of the most salient rules and concepts about retirement accounts, and then we'll give you an action guide. Specifically, we'll highlight a retirement account sequence based on your current situation. There is a sequence for you if you fall into any of these categories:

1. An employee (i.e., you receive an IRS Form W-2)
2. Self-employed, an independent contractor (i.e., you receive an IRS Form 1099), or unemployed
3. An employee (W-2) with a side hustle (1099)

The relevant section will tell you what to do first, second, and third. For example, if you are an employee and you want to contribute $1,000 to your retirement accounts this year, it likely will be most advantageous from a tax and economic perspective to simply put your $1,000 in your employer's 401(k) plan in order to get any 401(k) employer-matching money. But if you are an employee and you want to contribute, say, $50,000 to retirement accounts this year, you'll likely need to use not only your employer's 401(k) plan but also a Roth IRA, an HSA, and perhaps a taxable brokerage account because your savings goal is so large and retirement accounts have contribution limits.

THREE RETIREMENT ACCOUNT CONSIDERATIONS

The Roth Versus Traditional Debate

Roth and *traditional* are flavors of retirement accounts. You can think of them like chocolate and vanilla. Just like you can have a chocolate cake with chocolate icing or a chocolate cake with vanilla icing, you can also have a traditional 401(k) or a Roth 401(k). You can also have a traditional IRA or a Roth IRA. Both Roth and traditional accounts are tax advantaged and tax deferred, meaning that profits and earnings are not taxed as long as your money remains inside the retirement account. Throughout the retirement account sequences, you'll see that the Roth-style account tends to be favored. But before we get to that, let's clarify the two primary differences between Roth accounts and traditional accounts.

First, from a tax perspective, you get a deduction on your federal income tax return when you contribute to a traditional-style account but then pay income tax on the money when you take it out for retirement. A Roth-style account is the opposite. You don't get a tax deduction when you contribute to the account, but you can withdraw money tax-free for retirement (assuming Congress doesn't change the law). If your tax rate today is identical to your tax rate in retirement, then the traditional/Roth decision is a wash, as long as you contribute the same dollar amount to either type of account. If your tax rate in retirement is lower than it is today, then a traditional account will result in less tax overall. If your tax rate in retirement is higher than it is today, then a Roth account will put you ahead from a tax perspective. Unfortunately, it can be difficult to predict your tax rate in retirement, especially if retirement is many years away. The three biggest drivers of your tax rate in retirement are (1) whether your income goes up, down, or stays stable, (2) whether you move to a lower-tax state (the classic example being Florida), and (3) whether Congress raises income tax rates, lowers rates, or keeps them the same. Assuming your income and state of residence stay the same in retirement, then the biggest variable is congressional policy, which can be difficult to forecast.

Second, Roth accounts tend to have more flexible distribution rules. It's generally easier to pull some of your money out of a Roth account than out of a traditional account if you need that money before retirement age. For example, if you have a Roth IRA (not a Roth 401[k]), principal distributions are tax-free regardless of timing, and earnings distributions are tax-free after five years. Or, at the other end of the spectrum, if you have all the money you need for retirement and you want to continue to let your wealth grow tax-free inside the Roth account during retirement, that can be an option. Traditional IRAs have required minimum distributions, which means you have to take a certain amount of money out of the traditional IRA and pay tax on it during retirement. But Roth IRAs don't have any required minimum distributions, so you can let the money grow tax deferred inside the Roth IRA for your lifetime. Many people leave their Roth accounts untouched and let them pass to their children or heirs when they die, which is a tax-smart strategy. The longer that money stays inside a tax-deferred account and grows tax deferred, the greater the tax benefits.

My rule of thumb is to choose a Roth-style account whenever it's available because I want to protect myself against future tax rate increases and I like the distribution flexibility of a Roth.

Investment Flexibility Inside an Employer Plan

When you contribute money to an employer-sponsored retirement plan like a 401(k), 403(b), or 457(b) plan, you may find that your employer limits the types of investments you can make inside your account. For example, a 401(k) plan may have a set menu of fifteen investment funds that you can choose from, which can be rather limiting. If you find yourself with limited investment options, there are two things to try. First, you can call the company that holds your plan (e.g., Fidelity, Vanguard, ADP, T. Rowe Price, etc.) and ask the representative whether your employer's plan allows in-service distributions. An in-service distribution lets you roll your retirement money into an IRA while you're still working for the company. Once the money is inside your IRA, you have a broad range of investment options. Alternatively, if an in-service distribution isn't available, see whether the employer plan rules allow you to self-direct your retirement plan money. Self-direction can let you access a broader array of investment options inside your retirement plan. If you can't self-direct or distribute while in service, it probably still makes sense to contribute to your employer plan. Even though your investment options might be narrow, most employers will match your retirement contributions, and you don't want to leave this free matching money on the table.

Charitable Contributions from a Traditional IRA

If you are seventy and a half or older and have a traditional IRA (not a Roth IRA), you can donate money directly from your traditional IRA to a charity. The benefit is that you avoid the income tax that you would otherwise pay on the IRA distribution. This benefit is in addition to the tax deduction you received when you initially contributed the money to the traditional IRA, so that traditional IRA money is not taxed on contribution, growth, or distribution—a triple tax benefit.

THE RETIREMENT ACCOUNT SEQUENCES

If You Are an Employee: A Retirement Account Sequence

STEP 1: OPEN A RETIREMENT ACCOUNT WITH YOUR EMPLOYER

If your employer offers a retirement plan (e.g., a 401[k] plan, a 403[b] plan, a 457[b] plan, a SIMPLE IRA, a money purchase plan, or an ESOP) *and* your employer matches your contributions, then contribute enough money to get the matching dollars. For example, if you make $60,000 per year and your employer offers a 100 percent match up to 3 percent of your salary, that means that your employer will contribute $1 to your retirement plan for every dollar that you contribute, up to $1,800 (i.e., 3 percent of your $60,000 salary). So, step one in this example would be to contribute $1,800 to your employer's plan so that you get the full match and don't leave free money on the table.

STEP 2: MAX OUT A ROTH IRA

If you want to save more for retirement, the next step is to max out a Roth IRA. In 2025, you can contribute the lesser of (a) your salary or (b) $7,000 to a Roth IRA. If you are fifty or older on December 31, 2025, you can contribute the lesser of (a) your salary or (b) $8,000 to a Roth IRA. If you are married and file a joint federal income tax return with your spouse (i.e., you are married filing jointly), then you can treat your spouse's income as though it were your own salary; this is helpful if you make less than $7,000 or $8,000 of salary but you would still like to contribute the maximum amount to your own Roth IRA.

If you make too much money, the IRS says that you are not allowed to contribute to a Roth IRA. Specifically, for 2025, you cannot contribute to a Roth IRA if (a) you are married filing jointly or file as a qualified widow and the adjusted gross income on your tax return is $246,000 or more, (b) you file as single or as head of household and the adjusted gross income on your tax return is $165,000 or more, or (c) you file as married filing separately and the adjusted gross income on your tax return is $10,000 or more. Additionally, the amount you are allowed to contribute to a Roth IRA is partially reduced if (a) you are married filing jointly or file as a qualified widow and the adjusted gross income on your tax return is between $236,000 and $246,000, (b) you file as single or as head of household and the adjusted gross income on your tax return is between $150,000 and $165,000, or (c) you file as married filing separately and the adjusted gross income on your tax return is between $0 and $10,000. The partial reduction formula is a bit complicated, so you can use an online calculator to figure the amount.

But do not despair! If you make more than these threshold amounts, you can still contribute the full amount to your Roth IRA with the backdoor strategy. Here's the game plan: You contribute $7,000 (or $8,000, depending on your age) to a traditional IRA, keep the money in cash, wait about a month, and then transfer the $7,000 (or $8,000) of cash to a Roth IRA. There is no federal income tax when you roll the money from the traditional IRA to the Roth IRA because you did not deduct that traditional IRA contribution (i.e., the traditional IRA contribution was made with after-tax money). Although the IRS has not specifically sanctioned backdoor Roth IRAs and it may challenge the strategy, the backdoor Roth IRA is pretty widely used.

Be warned, however: If you have any money in traditional IRAs, the *pro rata rule* can trigger an unexpected surprise when you do a backdoor Roth IRA. The pro rata rule says that the IRS will look at all your traditional IRA money together. For example, let's say you have $93,000 in a traditional IRA, and you deducted all the contributions you made to that traditional IRA up to this point (i.e., all the money in the traditional IRA is before-tax money, not after-tax money). Then you do a backdoor Roth IRA with $7,000. The IRS will look at all your traditional IRA money together, and it will say that 93 percent of your total traditional IRA money is before-tax money and only 7 percent is after-tax money. Therefore, when you convert that $7,000 to a Roth IRA as part of your backdoor Roth strategy, 93 percent of the $7,000 (i.e., $6,510) will be taxed at ordinary income tax rates.

The solution here? Move that $93,000 of traditional IRA money into your 401(k) plan because the pro rata rule only applies to money in IRAs, not to money in 401(k)s. You will have to call your 401(k) plan administrator or check your plan documents to confirm that your 401(k) plan rules allow contributions from traditional IRAs. And if you cannot move your traditional IRA money into a 401(k), then honestly a backdoor Roth IRA probably doesn't make sense because it will be taxed.

STEP 3: TOP OFF YOUR EMPLOYER RETIREMENT PLAN

If you want to save even more for retirement, you can make

extra contributions to your retirement plan. As of 2025, you can add the following amounts:[1]

- For 401(k), 403(b), and 457(b) plans: the lesser of (a) 100 percent of your salary or (b) $23,500. If you are age fifty or older on December 31, 2025, then you can contribute the lesser of (a) 100 percent of your salary or (b) $31,000. And if you are sixty, sixty-one, sixty-two, or sixty-three, you can contribute $34,750.
- For SIMPLE 401(k) and SIMPLE IRA plans: $16,500. (If your employer meets certain requirements, this number may be increased to $17,600.) If you are fifty or older on December 31, 2025, you can contribute $20,000. And if you are sixty, sixty-one, sixty-two, or sixty-three, you can contribute $21,750.
- For SARSEPs: the lesser of (a) 25 percent of your salary or (b) $23,500. If you are fifty or older on December 31, 2025, you can contribute an

---

1. One thing to be aware of: If you switch jobs midyear, excess retirement plan contributions are a very common pitfall. Usually, your employer will automatically stop your retirement plan contributions once you reach the annual limit for that year. But if you contribute to a retirement account with employer number 1 and then switch jobs and join employer number 2, employer number 2 doesn't know how much you contributed to your retirement plan with employer number 1. This means that you could contribute too much money to your second retirement account that year. For example, let's say your 401(k) contribution limit for the year is $23,500. You contribute $20,000 to your 401(k) with employer 1. Then you switch jobs in October and contribute 10 percent of your salary each month to your 401(k) with employer 2. Let's say that 10 percent ends up meaning that you have contributed $6,000 to your 401(k) with employer 2. You have contributed $26,000 to 401(k) plans for the year, and you have an excess 401(k) contribution of $2,500 for the year. The result is that the IRS will tax you heavily on the $2,500 if you don't withdraw the money by the excess contribution deadline, which is generally April 15 of the following year.

additional $7,500, regardless of whether you
have enough salary (i.e., the 25 percent salary limit doesn't apply to the $7,500 additional
contribution).

STEP 4: ADD AFTER-TAX CONTRIBUTIONS
TO YOUR EMPLOYER PLAN

This is an option if you want to really put away a lot for retirement. If your employer plan is a 401(k), a 403(b), a SARSEP, or
an ESOP, ask your employer whether you can make after-tax
contributions. The term *after-tax contribution* is really a term
of art, and it's wildly confusing. Traditional 401(k) contributions are often called *pretax contributions* and Roth 401(k)
contributions are often called *after-tax contributions*. But here
in this step 4, when we talk about an after-tax contribution, it's
neither a traditional or a Roth contribution but rather something else entirely. Here, after-tax contribution refers to a way
to supercharge the amount you put into your employer's retirement plan. Specifically, the IRS says that the total plan contribution limit for 2025 is the lesser of (a) 100 percent of your
salary or (b) $70,000. If you are fifty or older on December 31,
2025, you can contribute the lesser of (a) 100 percent of your
salary or (b) $77,500. And if you are sixty, sixty-one, sixty-two,
or sixty-three, you can contribute $81,250.

For example, let's say you make $200,000 per year. You
contribute $23,500 to your 401(k), and your employer contrib-
utes a 4 percent match of $8,000. If the rules of your employer's
401(k) plan allow for after-tax contributions, then the IRS will
let you contribute an additional $38,500 to your 401(k) (i.e.,
$70,000 minus the $23,500 you've already contributed and the
$8,000 your employer contributed).

STEP 5: OPEN A BROKERAGE ACCOUNT

After you have maxed out all the tax-advantaged accounts, you can put any additional savings into a normal brokerage account.

If You Are Self-Employed, Are an Independent Contractor, or Are Unemployed: A Retirement Account Sequence

STEP 1: MAX OUT A ROTH IRA

First, max out a Roth IRA. In 2025, you can contribute the lesser of (a) the amount of your self-employment income or (b) $7,000 to a Roth IRA. If you are fifty or older on December 31, 2025, you can contribute the lesser of (a) your self-employment income or (b) $8,000 to a Roth IRA. Self-employment income is the amount of income that you pay federal payroll tax on (e.g., FICA and FUTA). If you are married and file a joint federal income tax return with your spouse (i.e., you are married filing jointly), then you can treat your spouse's income as though it were your own salary; this is helpful if you make less than $7,000 or $8,000 of salary but you would still like to contribute the maximum amount to your own Roth IRA.

If you make too much money, the IRS says that you are not allowed to contribute to a Roth IRA. Specifically, for 2025, you cannot contribute to a Roth IRA if (a) you are married filing jointly or file as a qualified widow and the adjusted gross income on your tax return is $246,000 or more, (b) you file as single or as head of household and the adjusted gross income on your tax return is $165,000 or more, or (c) you file as married filing separately and the adjusted gross income on your tax return is $10,000 or more. Additionally, the amount you are allowed to contribute to a Roth IRA is partially reduced if (a) you are married filing jointly or file as a qualified widow and the adjusted gross income on your tax return is between $236,000 and $246,000, (b) you file as single or as head of household and the adjusted gross income on your tax return is between $150,000 and $165,000, or (c) you file as married filing separately and the adjusted gross income on your tax return is between $0 and $10,000. The partial reduction formula is a bit complicated, so you can use an online calculator to figure the amount.

But do not despair! If you make more than these threshold amounts, you can still contribute the full amount to your Roth IRA with the backdoor strategy. Here's the game plan: You contribute $7,000 (or $8,000, depending on your age) to a traditional IRA, keep the money in cash, wait about a month, and then transfer the $7,000 (or $8,000) of cash to a Roth IRA. There is no federal income tax when you roll the money from the traditional IRA to the Roth IRA because you did not deduct that traditional IRA contribution (i.e., the traditional IRA contribution was made with after-tax money). Although the IRS has not specifically sanctioned backdoor Roth IRAs and it may challenge the strategy, the backdoor Roth IRA is pretty widely used.

Be warned, however: If you have any money in traditional IRAs, the *pro rata rule* can trigger a surprise when you do a backdoor Roth IRA. The pro rata rule says that the IRS will look at all your traditional IRA money together. For example, let's say you have $93,000 in a traditional IRA, and you deducted all the contributions you made to that traditional IRA up to this point (i.e., all the money in the traditional IRA is before-tax money, not after-tax money). Then you do a backdoor Roth IRA with $7,000. The IRS will look at all your traditional IRA money together, and it will say that 93 percent of your total traditional IRA money is before-tax money and only

7 percent is after-tax money. Therefore, when you convert that $7,000 to a Roth IRA as part of your backdoor Roth strategy, 93 percent of the $7,000 (i.e., $6,510) will be taxed at ordinary income tax rates.

The solution here? Move that $93,000 of traditional IRA money into your 401(k) plan because the pro rata rule only applies to money in IRAs, not to money in 401(k)s. You will have to call your 401(k) plan administrator or check your plan documents to confirm that your 401(k) plan rules allow contributions from traditional IRAs. And if you cannot move your traditional IRA money into a 401(k), then honestly a backdoor Roth IRA probably doesn't make sense because it will be taxed.

STEP 2: OPEN A ROTH SOLO 401(K)

A Roth Solo 401(k) plan can cover you and your spouse if you work together in the same business. A 401(k) provider like Vanguard or Fidelity can help you set up a Roth Solo 401(k) pretty easily. In 2025, you and your spouse each can contribute the lesser of (a) 100 percent of your self-employment income or (b) $70,000. If you are fifty or older on December 31, 2025, you can contribute the lesser of (a) 100 percent of your self-employment income or (b) $77,500. When you set up your Roth Solo 401(k), make sure the plan documents allow contributions from traditional IRAs, as this can help enable future backdoor Roth contributions.

Keep in mind that if you (or you and your spouse) hire employees in the future, you will have to convert your Roth Solo 401(k) plan to a standard Roth 401(k) plan because the IRS's 401(k) nondiscrimination rules say that your 401(k) plan must cover almost all employees. The benefit here is that a 401(k) plan can help you attract employees; the drawback is that you must do annual nondiscrimination testing (i.e., pay your 401(k) provider to run complicated calculations for you). You might also have to contribute to your employees' 401(k) accounts if they are not contributing enough.

STEP 3: OPEN A BROKERAGE ACCOUNT

After you have maxed out all the tax-advantaged accounts, you can put any additional savings into a normal brokerage account.

If your business is large or grows significantly, you can consider adding a pension plan (a.k.a. a *defined benefit plan*) or a profit-sharing plan to provide additional retirement savings for you and your employees. But those are major business decisions that require more detailed analysis.

If You Are an Employee with a Side Hustle: A Retirement Account Sequence

STEP 1: OPEN A RETIREMENT ACCOUNT WITH YOUR EMPLOYER

If your employer offers a retirement plan (e.g., a 401[k] plan, a 403[b] plan, a 457[b] plan, a SIMPLE IRA, a money purchase plan, or an ESOP) *and* your employer matches your contributions, then contribute enough money to get the matching dollars. For example, if you make $60,000 per year and your employer offers a 100 percent match up to 3 percent of your salary, that means that your employer will contribute $1 to your retirement plan for every dollar that you contribute, up to $1,800 (i.e., 3 percent of your $60,000 salary). So, step one in this example would be to contribute $1,800 to your employer's plan so that you get the full match and don't leave free money on the table.

STEP 2: MAX OUT A ROTH IRA

If you want to save more for retirement, the next step is to max out a Roth IRA. In 2025, you can contribute the lesser of (a) your salary or (b) $7,000 to a Roth IRA. If you are fifty or older on December 31, 2025, you can contribute the lesser of (a) your salary or (b) $8,000 to a Roth IRA. If you are married and file a joint federal income tax return with your spouse (i.e., you are married filing jointly), then you can treat your spouse's income as though it were your own salary; this is helpful if you make less than $7,000 or $8,000 of salary but you would still like to contribute the maximum amount to your own Roth IRA.

If you make too much money, the IRS says that you are not allowed to contribute to a Roth IRA. Specifically, for 2025, you cannot contribute to a Roth IRA if (a) you are married filing jointly or file as a qualified widow and the adjusted gross income on your tax return is $246,000 or more, (b) you file as single or as head of household and the adjusted gross income on your tax return is $165,000 or more, or (c) you file as married filing separately and the adjusted gross income on your tax return is $10,000 or more. Additionally, the amount you are allowed to contribute to a Roth IRA is partially reduced if (a) you are married filing jointly or file as a qualified widow and the adjusted gross income on your tax return is between $236,000 and $246,000, (b) you file as single or as head of household and the adjusted gross income on your tax return is between $150,000 and $165,000, or (c) you file as married filing separately and the adjusted gross income on your tax return is between $0 and $10,000. The partial reduction formula is a bit complicated, so you can use an online calculator to figure the amount.

But do not despair! If you make more than these threshold amounts, you can still contribute the full amount to your

Roth IRA with the backdoor strategy. Here's the game plan: You contribute $7,000 (or $8,000, depending on your age) to a traditional IRA, keep the money in cash, wait about a month, and then transfer the $7,000 (or $8,000) of cash to a Roth IRA. There is no federal income tax when you roll the money from the traditional IRA to the Roth IRA because you did not deduct that traditional IRA contribution (i.e., the traditional IRA contribution was made with after-tax money). Although the IRS has not specifically sanctioned backdoor Roth IRAs and it may challenge the strategy, the backdoor Roth IRA is pretty widely used.

Be warned, however: If you have any money in traditional IRAs, the *pro rata rule* can trigger a surprise when you do a backdoor Roth IRA. The pro rata rule says that the IRS will look at all your traditional IRA money together. For example, let's say you have $93,000 in a traditional IRA, and you deducted all the contributions you made to that traditional IRA up to this point (i.e., all the money in the traditional IRA is before-tax money, not after-tax money). Then you do a backdoor Roth IRA with $7,000. The IRS will look at all your traditional IRA money together, and it will say that 93 percent of your total traditional IRA money is before-tax money and only 7 percent is after-tax money. Therefore, when you convert that $7,000 to a Roth IRA as part of your backdoor Roth strategy, 93 percent of the $7,000 (i.e., $6,510) will be taxed at ordinary income tax rates.

The solution here? Move that $93,000 of traditional IRA money into your 401(k) plan because the pro rata rule only applies to money in IRAs, not to money in 401(k)s. You will have to call your 401(k) plan administrator or check your plan documents to confirm that your 401(k) plan rules allow contributions from traditional IRAs. And if you cannot move your traditional IRA money into a 401(k), then honestly a backdoor Roth IRA probably doesn't make sense because it will be taxed.

STEP 3: TOP OFF YOUR EMPLOYER RETIREMENT PLAN

If you want to save even more for retirement, you can make extra contributions to your retirement plan. As of 2025, you can add the following amounts:[2]

- For 401(k), 403(b), and 457(b) plans: the lesser of (a) 100 percent of your salary or (b) $23,500. If you are age fifty or older on December 31, 2025, then you can contribute the lesser of (a) 100 percent of your salary or (b) $31,000. And if you are sixty, sixty-one, sixty-two, or sixty-three, you can contribute $34,750.
- For SIMPLE 401(k) and SIMPLE IRA plans: $16,500. (If your employer meets certain requirements, this number may be increased to $17,600.) If you are fifty or older on December 31, 2025, you can contribute $20,000. And if you are sixty, sixty-one, sixty-two, or sixty-three, you can contribute $21,750.

---

2. One thing to be aware of: If you switch jobs midyear, excess retirement plan contributions are a very common pitfall. Usually, your employer will automatically stop your retirement plan contributions once you reach the annual limit for that year. But if you contribute to a retirement account with employer number 1 and then switch jobs and join employer number 2, employer number 2 doesn't know how much you contributed to your retirement plan with employer number 1. This means that you could contribute too much money to your second retirement account that year. For example, let's say your 401(k) contribution limit for the year is $23,500. You contribute $20,000 to your 401(k) with employer 1. Then you switch jobs in October and contribute 10 percent of your salary each month to your 401(k) with employer 2. Let's say that 10 percent ends up meaning that you have contributed $6,000 to your 401(k) with employer 2. You have contributed $26,000 to 401(k) plans for the year, and you have an excess 401(k) contribution of $2,500 for the year. The result is that the IRS will tax you heavily on the $2,500 if you don't withdraw the money by the excess contribution deadline, which is generally April 15 of the following year.

- For SARSEPs: the lesser of (a) 25 percent of your salary or (b) $23,500. If you are fifty or older on December 31, 2025, you can contribute an additional $7,500, regardless of whether you have enough salary (i.e., the 25 percent salary limit doesn't apply to the $7,500 additional contribution).

STEP 4: ADD AFTER-TAX CONTRIBUTIONS TO YOUR EMPLOYER PLAN

This is an option if you want to really put away a lot for retirement. If your employer plan is a 401(k), a 403(b), a SARSEP, or an ESOP, ask your employer whether you can make after-tax contributions. The term *after-tax contribution* is really a term of art, and it's wildly confusing. Traditional 401(k) contributions are often called *pretax contributions* and Roth 401(k) contributions are often called *after-tax contributions*. But here in this step 4, when we talk about an after-tax contribution, it's neither a traditional or a Roth contribution but rather something else entirely. Here, *after-tax contribution* refers to a way to supercharge the amount you put into your employer's retirement plan. Specifically, the IRS says that the total plan contribution limit for 2025 is the lesser of (a) 100 percent of your salary or (b) $70,000. If you are fifty or older on December 31, 2025, you can contribute the lesser of (a) 100 percent of your salary or (b) $77,500. And if you are sixty, sixty-one, sixty-two, or sixty-three, you can contribute $81,250.

For example, let's say you make $200,000 per year. You contribute $23,500 to your 401(k), and your employer contributes a 4 percent match of $8,000. If the rules of your employer's 401(k) plan allow for after-tax contributions, then the IRS will let you contribute an additional $38,500 to your 401(k) (i.e.,

$70,000 minus the $23,500 you've already contributed and the $8,000 your employer contributed).

STEP 5: OPEN A SEP ROTH IRA

The SEP Roth IRA is unique because it is the only retirement plan that plays well with other retirement plans. Usually, the $70,000 annual contribution limit applies no matter how many plans you have. In other words, even if you had ten different 401(k) plans, you couldn't stuff $700,000 into retirement accounts in 2025. But the SEP IRA is the exception to this combined-limit rule. Even if there is $70,000 going into your 401(k), you still can contribute the lesser of (a) 25 percent of your compensation or (b) $70,000 to your SEP Roth IRA. So, in theory, you could stuff $140,000 into tax-advantaged retirement plans in 2025! This is a huge tax advantage.

If your employer already offers a SEP IRA, then you can reverse this advice and set up your own Roth Solo 401(k). *See the section titled "If You Are Self-Employed, Are an Independent Contractor, or Are Unemployed: A Retirement Account Sequence" for more information.*

STEP 6: OPEN A BROKERAGE ACCOUNT

After you have maxed out all the tax-advantaged accounts, you can put any additional savings into a normal brokerage account.

THE BOTTOM LINE

This chapter is one way to put the pieces together and optimize your retirement account structure. As you can probably tell, it can be a bit of a puzzle to figure out how retirement accounts interact and play together. Hopefully these proposed sequences will give you the clarity you need to move forward with setting up your investment-account structure.

CHAPTER 9

Fund Educational Goals

Education savings accounts have evolved over the years. Today there are six common vehicles that people use to house education savings:

- A brokerage account
- Series EE and series I government bonds
- A Coverdell ESA
- A UTMA custodial account
- A Roth IRA
- A Section 529 plan

We will explore each of these options in some detail, but we'll focus a lot of our time on the 529 plan. The 529 plan is by far the most popular choice today because it has the strongest tax advantages and the highest contribution limits. Contribution limits matter because education can be expensive! That said, the investment options inside a 529 plan can be quite limited, so unless you're committed to a purely passive investment approach, a normal taxable brokerage account or UTMA could also be worth consideration.

BROKERAGE ACCOUNT

A taxable brokerage account is often a default option. If you are paying for preschool, K–12 education, college, graduate school, or other types of programs or extracurriculars out of pocket, you might dip into your long-term savings and investments inside your normal taxable investment account. Alternatively, you can open a savings account or brokerage account that is dedicated to education savings. Earmarking money for education and segregating it in its own account can trigger mental accounting and give you peace of mind that you are putting enough money aside.

SERIES EE AND SERIES I BONDS

Series EE and series I bonds are savings bonds issued by the US government (more on bonds, a type of investment, in part 3). Generally, if you cash out a series EE or series I bond today and you use the proceeds to pay for higher education expenses, then you don't pay any federal income tax on the interest that you earn on that bond. There are a lot of rules and restrictions. For example, the bond must be issued after 1989, you must cash out the bond in the same year you pay for the education expenses, your education expenses must meet the definition of "qualified higher education expenses," the expenses must be paid to an eligible educational institution, and the modified adjusted gross income (MAGI) on your federal income tax return must be less than the threshold. In 2025, the threshold is $114,500 for single filers and $179,250 for married couples who file a joint federal income tax return.

The myriad tax rules and restrictions aside, another issue with series EE and series I bonds for higher education is that they are an investment first and a tax-advantaged savings strategy second. This means that from an investment perspective, series EE and series I bonds may not make sense. The rate of return on the bonds might be lower than what you could get on other investments. So you may very well decide that it's best to skip these bonds, despite the fact that the interest could be tax-free if you redeem the bond to pay for higher education.

COVERDELL ESA

A Coverdell ESA is like an IRA account but for education. Money inside the account grows tax deferred and distributions from the account are tax-free as long as they are for qualified education expenses of the ESA's beneficiary. *Qualified education expenses* in the ESA context include not only certain higher education expenses, but also certain K–12 expenses. One downside is that contributions to an ESA are limited to $2,000 per year. And this $2,000 cap is reduced if you make more than the income threshold. Specifically, for 2025, single filers who have between $95,000 and $110,000 of MAGI on their federal income tax return can contribute some fraction of $2,000 to a Coverdell ESA, and cannot contribute to an ESA at all if MAGI is $110,000 or more. These thresholds are $190,000 to $220,000 for married couples who file a joint federal income tax return. Coverdell ESAs do have a broad range of investment options and can be worth further consideration if you're looking to put aside $2,000 or less for K–12 or higher education each year.

UTMA CUSTODIAL ACCOUNT

The Uniform Transfers to Minors Act (UTMA) is a model law written in the 1980s. Almost all US states have adopted some version of this model law as their own state law. UTMA accounts are not specific to education or college savings. Instead, any money deposited into the account is considered a gift to the child (i.e., a minor) for whom the account was set up. Money inside the UTMA account must be used for the benefit of the minor, and when the minor reaches adulthood (generally age eighteen or twenty-one, depending on state law), the money is theirs to access and use free and clear. (A scary thought for some parents of eighteen-year-olds!)

From a federal income tax perspective, the UTMA account is neither tax advantaged nor tax deferred. Contributions and distributions are taxed, and growth inside the account is also taxed. However, those earnings and gains inside the account are taxed at the minor's tax rate, which often is lower than the tax rate of the parent or adult who contributes to the UTMA account. Also, investment options are generally quite broad inside a UTMA account. Although the UTMA doesn't have many tax advantages, it can be an easy way to set up a trust fund for a child without actually doing the work of setting up a trust (i.e., hiring a lawyer to draft trust documents). It can also make sense if you are uncertain about whether your child will go to private school or college or not—because again, the child can use the money for any purpose at age eighteen or twenty-one.

ROTH IRA

Although a Roth IRA is a retirement savings account, it is possible to tap into a Roth IRA to pay for higher education. As mentioned in chapter 8 on retirement accounts, you can with-draw your principal (i.e., your original contributions) from your Roth IRA at any time without taxes or penalties. From there, you can withdraw the earnings (i.e., the profits on your prin-cipal) without any taxes or penalties after age fifty-nine and a half, as long as you made your first contribution to the Roth IRA at least five years ago. So, from a tax perspective, people over the age of fifty-nine and a half could consider using their Roth IRA retirement accounts to fund college for themselves or their children or grandchildren. That said, from an economic perspective, you never want to jeopardize your own retirement or financial security, even for the sake of your children or for education. So the nontax implications of using a Roth IRA for higher education also warrant some consideration.

If you are under age fifty-nine and a half and you with-draw earnings from your Roth IRA to pay for certain qualified higher education expenses, then the earnings will be taxed, but the 10 percent early withdrawal penalty will not apply. For example, let's say you deposit $100 into your Roth IRA, invest the money, and earn $40 on your investments. Your Roth IRA account balance is now $140, and you are fifty-eight years old. If you withdraw the full $140, you would normally pay taxes and a 10 percent penalty on the $40. If we assume an effec-tive tax rate of 30 percent for the sake of this example, that means that 40 percent (i.e., 30 percent plus 10 percent) of the $40, or $16, will go to the federal government, leaving you with $124 of your original $140. But if you use the money to pay for qualified higher education expenses, then, in our example, you only pay the 30 percent tax and not the 10 percent penalty. You would pay $12 of tax and retain $128 of your original $140. That is the special exception to the Roth IRA rules for higher education that you'll often see cited. Again, the nontax impli-cations of using a Roth IRA for higher education also warrant some consideration.

Bottom line: It is possible to withdraw principal and, under the right circumstances, earnings from your Roth IRA to fund education. But a Roth IRA is first and foremost a retirement account. If you are torn about whether to use a Roth IRA to house your nest egg or to house college savings, it probably makes the most sense to use the Roth IRA for the nest egg and to use an education-specific plan for education.

529 PLAN

To help any children in your life pay for college—whether they are your own kids, members of your extended family, or even outside your family—you can set up a unique 529 plan for each child. If the child does not use all the money in their 529 plan, you can roll the money into the 529 plan of another child. Alternatively, according to the SECURE 2.0 Act (passed in 2022), you can roll up to $35,000 of leftover 529 plan money into a Roth IRA for the benefit of the child who was the designated beneficiary of the 529 plan if (a) the 529 plan has been in existence for at least fifteen years, (b) the rolled over money wasn't added to the 529 plan in the last five years, and (c) contributions to the Roth IRA from any source don't exceed the annual IRA contribution limits, plus (d) any other restrictions that the Treasury Department might specify by regulation.

In 2025, an individual can contribute up to $95,000 to any given 529 plan without triggering federal gift tax (and a married couple can contribute up to $190,000).[1] The money inside the 529 plan grows tax deferred, which means that profits and earnings are not taxed as long as your money remains

---

1.   Note that you will need to file a federal gift tax return on IRS Form 709 each year for five years if you "superfund" a 529 plan account. Even though you won't owe gift tax, the IRS still wants you to report the contribution.

inside the 529 plan account. And you can withdraw the money tax-free to pay for tuition, room and board, and certain other required expenses at college. You can also withdraw up to $10,000 per year from the 529 plan to pay for K–12 tuition at a public, private, or religious school. (But because this $10,000 rule is a federal rule, it's also important to check the rules in your particular state. In some states, there could be a recapture of state income tax benefits or other penalties if you use 529 funds for K–12 tuition.) Finally, you can withdraw money tax-free to pay for certain federally designated apprenticeship programs. As mentioned previously, the most significant issue with a 529 plan is that the investment choices inside the plan are typically limited to a select menu of mutual funds, exchange-traded funds (ETFs), or pre-allocated portfolios.

Many people wonder whether they can use a 529 plan to fund education expenses for themselves. The answer is yes, you can. That said, the big benefit of a 529 plan is that the investments inside the plan grow tax deferred, so it generally doesn't make sense to set up a 529 plan if you are going to pull the money out shortly after contributing it. This is because the hassle of setting up the plan doesn't outweigh the benefit of tax deferral if the money only lives in the account for a short time. The exception to this rule? If you live in a state that offers a state income tax deduction for 529 plan contributions, it can make sense to contribute to a 529 plan, get the state tax deduction, and then immediately pull the money out to pay for education expenses. Many people do this for K–12 tuition for their kids too.

CONCLUDING THOUGHTS

A 529 plan is the first place to look for tax-advantaged education funding. It can be used for a wide variety of education (e.g., K–12, apprenticeships, and college). And although the investment options inside a 529 plan can be rather limited, the contribution limits are high, which means you can actually put enough away every year to fund even the most expensive educational goals. The Coverdell ESA is also a dedicated educational account, with broader investment options but more modest annual contribution limits. And don't rule out a traditional taxable brokerage account or even a UTMA for education savings. Although these accounts are not tax advantaged, they do offer a broader range of investment options than most 529 plans. Brokerage accounts and UTMAs may also offer more investment flexibility. Many 529 plan rules say that you can only buy or sell investments every, say, six months. But if the economic environment changes and you'd like to adjust your investment mix to keep with the changing times, you could find yourself stuck in investments you don't like. (More on economic environments in part 3.)

The final consideration is financial aid. The US federal government, and each specific school, writes its own rules and guidelines about financial aid and scholarships, and these rules and guidelines change rather frequently. So there are no hard-and-fast rules about which type of educational savings account is best from a financial aid perspective. But, as a general rule, you'll want to think about whether the assets in the educational savings account are considered the student's assets or the contributor's (e.g., parents' or grandparents') assets. If the assets in the account are considered the student's assets, the student might have a harder time qualifying for financial aid or scholarships because the formulas assume that the student doesn't need help paying for school. Assets in the parents' names can also reduce aid eligibility, but typically not by as much.

CHAPTER 10

Pay for Healthcare

Health savings accounts (HSAs) and health flexible spending arrangements (FSAs) both offer tax-advantaged ways to pay for healthcare. An HSA can be a helpful way to earmark money for future healthcare expenses, while an FSA can be helpful for more immediate expenses.

THE HEALTH SAVINGS ACCOUNT

Many employers offer HSAs as an employee benefit, but you can also set one up independently, regardless of your employment status. Specifically, if you (a) are not eligible for Medicare (i.e., generally, you are under age sixty-five) and (b) have high-deductible health insurance, you can contribute to an HSA. For 2025, high-deductible health insurance means an individual plan that has a deductible of $1,650 or more and a max out-of-pocket of $8,300 or less. Or it's a family plan that has a deductible of $3,300 or more and a max out-of-pocket of $16,600 or less.

You get a tax deduction for the amount that you contribute to the HSA each year. Then you can withdraw money from the HSA at any age to pay for medical expenses (these withdrawals are tax-free), or you can wait until age sixty-five and withdraw money from the HSA for any reason, medical or nonmedical. You will pay regular income tax on money that you withdraw after age sixty-five if you do not use it for medical purposes, but there is no tax penalty.

Growth inside the HSA is tax deferred until you withdraw it, so the HSA essentially functions like a secret traditional IRA. If you have individual insurance coverage, you can contribute up to $4,300 to an HSA in 2025. If you have family insurance coverage, you can contribute up to $8,550 to an HSA in 2025. And if you set up your HSA as a brokerage account rather than as a savings account, you should have some good investment options inside the HSA.

A HEALTH FLEXIBLE SPENDING ARRANGEMENT

A health FSA is a workplace benefit offered by some employers. You can choose to contribute money to your FSA each pay period, and your employer will deduct that money from your paycheck and put it into your FSA account. For 2025, the IRS says that you cannot contribute more than $3,300 a year to your FSA, and your specific employer plan may have a lower limit.

With FSAs, you generally "use it or lose it" every year. Some plans have a two-and-a-half-month grace period or a limited amount of money that you can carry over to the next plan year. But it's important to think realistically about how much you'll be spending on healthcare that year. This can be tricky because healthcare is, by nature, unpredictable; no one plans to get sick or injured. It's also important to know that your plan may not let you change the amount of your annual contribution once you have set it for that year. And if you overfund your FSA, there is a tendency to spend the money on things you don't actually need at the end of the year, just because you'll forfeit the money unless you do spend it.

From a federal income tax perspective, the benefit of an FSA is that you won't owe any federal income taxes or pay-roll taxes on the money you contribute to the account. Your employer may also put some money into your FSA account to help defray your healthcare costs. These contributions from your employer are also tax-free. Finally, if you spend the money in your FSA on qualified medical expenses, you don't pay any federal income tax on those FSA withdrawals. Health insurance premiums unfortunately are not qualified medical expenses, but a wide variety of other expenses, ranging from acupuncture to doctor-recommended wigs, do qualify. IRS Publication 502 has more details about qualified expenses.

CHAPTER 11

Manage Your Risk

Our account structure so far doesn't include an emergency fund. Many financial planning programs tell you to set aside a three-to-six-month rainy-day fund. The problem with this advice, however, is that it's not tailored to your unique situation. Rather than setting aside a random amount of cash for unspecified risks, it makes sense to get granular about the risks that are unique to you.

- I crash my car.
- I get sick.
- I become permanently disabled.
- I die.
- My partner dies.
- My parent/kid/spouse/dog/cat/friend gets really sick.

- My house burns down / floods / gets hit by hurricane.
- My identity gets stolen.
- I lose my job.
- I want a divorce.
- My partner wants a divorce.
- My partner wants a divorce (and hides all our money in offshore accounts).
- My taxes get audited and I owe money.
- I get sued.
- My fridge / water heater dies.
- My computer / cell phone dies.
- My bank accounts get hacked.
- Giant pythons attack me in my sleep.
- And more . . .

Next, take a look at each risk and list a possible solution for each one. Risk management solutions generally fall into three categories.

The first option is to simply accept the risk. If the risk is (a) very unlikely or (b) very low impact, then you can probably write "Do nothing" next to it. For example, if you live in the desert and there hasn't been a flood in two hundred years, you probably don't need flood insurance for your home. Or if your jean jacket is stolen at a baseball game, you probably just accept the risk and go buy a new jacket. Or if you lose your job but your spouse makes a lot of money and is a supportive partner, you live off their income.

Alternatively, if the risk would be painful but manageable, you can self-insure by setting aside cash. For example, let's say your mom has been having some health problems and you think there's a good chance that you'll want to take three months off work to care for her in the next five years. Your job would let you take three months of family leave, but they wouldn't pay you. Maybe you set aside three months of living expenses in cash to cover this scenario. Or maybe your refrigerator is fifteen years old and you know you'll need a new one soon. Either way, it makes sense to set aside some cash.

It's also worthwhile to investigate whether your employer sponsors emergency savings accounts. Employees who make less than the threshold amount of money can store up to $2,500 in their emergency savings account, and the $2,500 limit will increase with inflation every year. Some employers may automatically enroll eligible employees in an emergency savings account plan for up to 3 percent of the employee's salary, meaning that the employer will automatically take money out of the employee's paycheck and put it in the employee's emergency savings account. Some employers may also offer an employer match, meaning, for example, that if the employee deposits $500 in an emergency account, the employer will also deposit $500 in the emergency account. If your employer offers an emergency savings account, it could be a good option to consider, depending on the details of the plan. One thing to consider is whether the amount you contribute to an emergency savings account reduces the amount that you are allowed to contribute to your 401(k), 403(b), or 457(b). If you were planning to max out your 401(k) or similar plan, then it could be best to not contribute to the emergency savings account because the 401(k)-style plan likely will have a broader range of investment options. Emergency savings accounts only allow you to hold cash-like investments.

The third option is to buy insurance. As a general rule, I recommend that you only buy insurance for risks that you would not be able to survive. For example, if you and your partner both work and you don't have kids or people who depend on you financially, you probably don't need life insurance. Your partner would be devastated if you died tomorrow, but they could continue working and afford the mortgage and the groceries. In this scenario, it makes sense to take the money you'd spend on life insurance every month and invest it instead. In contrast, if your partner depends on you financially, it probably makes sense to buy life insurance.

If you have a big salary and an extra, say, $5,000 in your checking account, you can select higher deductibles (the amount you pay before insurance kicks in) on your car, home, and health insurance policies. Let's say you back your car into a parking meter. It's $3,000 to fix your bumper. Your car insurance won't cover any of the repair cost because it's less than your $5,000 deductible. Fixing your bumper is certainly not fun, but it's a risk you can survive. So it's better to have a high-deductible car insurance policy and a lower monthly car insurance premium because you can invest the money that you're saving on premiums. Then again, if big insurance policies and low deductibles give you peace of mind, by all means go that route. There is certainly an authenticity component to risk management, and there are no right or wrong answers. If security, safety, stability, and peace are important to you, honor that and be a little more conservative in your approach to insurance and emergency savings. It really is all about trusting what seems right to you.

CHAPTER 12

Get Savvy About Debt

Debt is a double-edged sword.

On the one hand, a debt-free life is a sovereign life. No mortgage, no student loans, no credit card debt, no car payment means you have freedom. You can change directions on a dime. If you want to quit your job and meditate on a mountaintop full-time tomorrow, it's easier to do that without monthly principal and interest payments. On the other hand, there are two scenarios where debt can make economic sense. First, if the interest rate on your debt is less than the interest rate you earn on your investments, you can come out ahead financially by keeping the debt; second, inflation erodes the value of debt, so high-inflation environments make debt more attractive.

SCENARIO 1: YOUR DEBT HAS A LOWER INTEREST RATE THAN YOU EARN ON YOUR INVESTMENTS

In this scenario, we'll illustrate the concept of leverage. You can think of leverage as good debt. The idea of leverage is that you borrow money, you invest that borrowed money, and you earn more on your investments than you pay in interest to the bank (or person/entity) from whom you borrowed the money. For example, let's say you buy a condo for $250,000. You have $250,000 in the bank and could theoretically decide to pay cash for the condo, but you decide to take out a mortgage. You put 20 percent down on the condo, which means that you use $50,000 of your own cash to pay for the condo, and you borrow the other $200,000 from the bank. Your $200,000 mortgage on the condo is a thirty-year fixed-rate mortgage, and your interest rate is 5 percent. Your principal and interest payment on the mortgage is $1,074 every month (ignoring any taxes and fees for the sake of the example).

Fast-forward thirty-five years. You're still living in the condo. You took the $200,000 that you didn't spend on the house and invested it in the stock market, and you made 8 percent per year on your $200,000 stock investment (i.e., you got leverage). Your $200,000 is now worth $2.96 million. Let's also assume that your house appreciated at 8 percent per year every year. Your house is now worth $3.69 million, and your mortgage is fully paid off. So here you are thirty-five years later. You have $6.65 million total—about $3 million of stocks in the bank and a house worth about $3.7 million. Not bad! The fact that you earned 8 percent on your money while only paying 5 percent interest to the bank helped you come out ahead.

Now let's say that you had decided to pay cash for the house thirty-five long years ago. You put your full $250,000 into your condo. You also took the $1,074 that you would have spent on your mortgage and invested it diligently in the stock market every month. Again, both the stock market and the housing market appreciate at 8 percent annually in our example. At the end of thirty-five years, you have a fully paid-off house worth $3.69 million, just like before. But you only have $2.46 million in the bank, rather than $2.96 million. Why? Where is that extra $500K? Here, you weren't able to take advantage of the difference between the 5 percent interest you were paying to the bank and the 8 percent interest you earned in the stock market.

Again, the idea of leverage is that if you have the opportunity to "play with the bank's money" (i.e., $200,000 in our example), then you can come out ahead if you're able to earn more on that money than you are paying in interest. Leverage can be a powerful way to multiply your money, and it is why certain financial advisers (and probably some of your family members) encourage reasonable amounts of debt and borrowing. So it can make sense to borrow *if* you feel confident that the interest rate on your loan is safely below what you can make on your investments *and* if you're willing to invest the amount that you borrow, rather than spend it. That said, these are two big ifs. First, we never really know what the future rate of return on our investments is going to be. Investing involves risk, and no one can predict the future. And second, psychologically, it takes discipline to invest after taking out a large loan. In our example, it could be tempting to spend, rather than invest, your $200,000.

SCENARIO 2: INFLATION ERODES THE VALUE OF DEBT

Inflation is the second economic consideration around debt.

Inflation can erode the value of fixed-rate debt because the debt—the amount you owe—becomes less valuable and less expensive over time. To continue with the example from scenario 1, you again buy a condo today for $250,000 and you take out that same mortgage. You again put $50,000 down and borrow $200,000 from a bank and you take out a mortgage with a $1,074 monthly payment. Twenty-nine years from now, you will still be paying $1,074 per month on your fixed-rate mortgage. But let's say that inflation averages 4 percent over the next thirty years. This means that everything you're buying thirty years from now will potentially be three times more expensive than it is today, just by virtue of the 4 percent inflation. And yet, thirty years from now, your $1,074 mortgage is still going to be the same $1,074 per month, not $3,200 per month, which will make it feel like a bargain. So as inflation causes everything in your life to get more expensive and (ideally) also causes your income and paycheck to rise, your fixed monthly debt payments are only going to feel more manageable over time. Inflation reduces your purchasing power, but it also reduces the pain of your debt, especially if your income rises with inflation. The bottom line is that if you anticipate that inflation will be high, you might not want to be in any hurry to pay off fixed-rate debt. This is especially true if you anticipate that your salary or income will also rise with inflation.

THE TAKEAWAYS ON DEBT

As a general rule of thumb, there are two types of debt: "good" debt and "bad" debt. Good debt is debt with a low interest rate. Generally, this is your mortgage, your student loan payment, and perhaps your car payment. Bad debt is debt with a high interest rate. Typically, this is your credit card debt. If you have bad debt, it's best to pay it off as soon as you possibly can. Sadly, the interest rate is so high that you will be stuck in a debt hole forever unless you get ahead of it right now. And if you have good debt, you don't necessarily have to rush to pay it off, especially if you are making good returns on your investments or if the debt has a fixed interest rate and you expect there will be inflation going forward.

One caveat: Just because a debt is "good" doesn't necessarily mean you should take it on. Yes, debt can make economic sense when you can get leverage or outsmart inflation. But there is something very liberating about being debt-free. Before you borrow to make a major purchase like a condo, a car, or graduate school, use an online calculator to figure your estimated monthly payment. Sit with it and see how it feels.

For example, how does it feel to have an extra $1,000 per month of overhead expenses to pay for that new adventure van? Is it worth it, or does it make your finances feel uncomfortable and tight? Also, how will that overhead expense feel five years from now? So many people are looking to make changes in their lives, whether it's quitting a corporate job, spending more time with family, or simply having less stress. If you are hoping to create a major change in your life, it can be helpful to stay flexible and to keep your debt as low as possible. In other words, if you want life to look differently five years from now, consider whether you want to lock yourself into a monthly payment today. When it comes to new debt, it's easy to have buyer's remorse, so proceed with caution and honor that little voice that is your authenticity.

CHAPTER 13

Automate Your Transfers

Automatic transfers are beautiful in their power and simplicity. Theoretically, your spending should be the same regardless of whether you see $2,500 in your paycheck or $1,950 in your paycheck. But we know that doesn't *feel* true. And study after study has shown that if you see the money in your account, you will spend it. So, rather than white-knuckling a budget, make your saving and spending more effortless by automatically funneling your income to separate accounts: spending, saving, and taxes.

For example, let's say you have a one-year consulting contract with a client who pays you $10,000 every month. You can set up automatic transfers with your bank so that $1,300 per month goes into your tax account, $2,000 per month goes into your Roth IRA, and the other $6,700 goes into your checking account and is yours to spend freely. You won't be tempted to spend the $3,300 reserved for taxes and saving because, thanks to automatic transfers, that $3,300 will never appear in your checking account.

A similar logic applies with paychecks. Employers automatically withhold federal and state income taxes according to the instructions you give your human resources department on IRS Form W-4. Employers who offer retirement plans also give you a paycheck that is net of whatever retirement plan contribution percentage that you specify. For example, let's say you earn $8,000 of salary every month. You fill out IRS Form W-4 as well as a retirement plan contribution agreement on your first day of work. With these two forms, you told your employer to take, for example, (1) $1,400 out of your paycheck for taxes every month and (2) $1,600 (i.e., 20 percent of your salary) out of your paycheck for retirement every month. The paycheck you receive every two weeks is $2,500, and you can spend that money freely knowing your saving is automatic.

In short, organization is a surprisingly powerful financial tool. My hope is that these chapters have armed you with a better sense of the types of accounts that you need to match and meet your specific financial goals. By closing old accounts, opening new accounts, and funding existing accounts, the research says you can save and spend with more ease.

PART 3

Investing

The third step of the financial planning process is to invest.

Investing is terrifying. Today's leading financial theories, including modern portfolio theory, the capital asset pricing model, and the efficient market hypothesis all assume that asset prices follow a normal distribution. Normal distributions are the bell curves you may have studied if you took a statistics class. The problem with these theories is that they underestimate the amount of risk in the stock market and in other financial markets. You probably don't need a lengthy mathematical explanation to validate what you know intuitively: investing is really risky. We're told to just put our money in the stock market and wait twenty years. It all works out in the end, they say. Or to just invest our 401(k) money in an index fund. Don't worry if it drops—it will recover eventually. Then we live in limbo. We know that investing can be a powerful way to compound our money and to have more space to live a life we love. But we need a road map so we can be confident we're making good investment decisions.

There are a million approaches to investing. Some people day-trade. Some people use computerized high-frequency trading, where they place thousands of trades every day for small profits or losses. Some people use passive index funds exclusively, while others use artificial intelligence to make their investment decisions. Some people buy only real estate because they like tangible investments.

Part 3 outlines a two-tiered approach to investing. First, look at the economic landscape in the country where you are considering an investment and allocate your money according to the current and anticipated economic climate. Second, find companies and projects that are making good money by doing good things in the world and put your money behind them. Finally, monitor and adjust if and when things change, either in the economy, in the business, or in your life.

Let's dive in.

CHAPTER 14

Find Your Motivation

It's natural to wonder what your financial future will hold. How much money do you need to have in the bank before you never have to worry about money again? When can you retire? Forty? Seventy? When are you financially free? How much money do you want to aim to have before work becomes optional, not mandatory? When can you have "eff-you money"? What is eff-you money? What is your personal amount—your "number"? How much is enough?

These are all perfectly appropriate financial planning questions. After all, earning income and amassing wealth is not something we do for the sake of it. It's something we do so that we can move through the world authentically and in alignment with our soul's true purpose. Having money in the bank gives us latitude to dance with the universe—to do the co-creative dance. Having our "number" in the bank gives us the widest degree of latitude, and it is natural to contemplate that number.

There are two mathematical answers to "What's my number?": a shorthand mathematical answer and a longhand mathematical answer.

The shorthand mathematical answer is the 4 percent rule of thumb. This widely accepted rule was developed in the mid-1990s by William Bengen, a financial adviser in California who looked at economic conditions from 1926 to 1976 (a fifty-year period that included the Great Depression and the post–World War II boom). He concluded that retirees who withdraw 4 percent of their portfolio with an inflation adjustment every year can live for at least thirty-three years without running out of money.

For example, let's say you're fifty years old. You look at a life expectancy table online. It says you can expect to live to age eighty-two, which seems like a reasonable number given your personal health and family history. You have $1 million in your Roth IRA, and you decide to retire. On January 1, your first day of retirement, you transfer $40,000 cash from your Roth IRA to your checking account, and that $40,000 is yours to spend freely that year. Over the course of that first year of retirement, the $960,000 left in your Roth IRA grows to $1,036,800 because it's a good year for the markets and you invested well. So on January 1 of your second year of retirement, the 4 percent rule says that you can transfer 4 percent of $1,036,800, or $41,472, to your checking account. That $41,472 is yours to spend freely in your second year of retirement, which is good because inflation has probably increased the cost of your groceries, utilities, and more.

The bottom line is that the 4 percent rule can help you determine your fixed annual income if you were to retire tomorrow, based on how much you have in your retirement accounts today. If, for example, you currently have $500,000 in retirement, the 4 percent rule says that lump sum could generate $20,000 per year for at least thirty-three years. You can also work backward, using the 4 percent rule as a tool to determine how much you need to save based on how much you want to spend once you're retired. For example, if you want to spend $200,000 each year in retirement, type "200,000 ÷ 0.04" into a calculator, and the 4 percent rule tells you that you need $5 million in the bank to generate $200,000 of income for at least thirty-three years.

The longhand mathematical answer to "What's my number?" is that it depends on ten different factors:

1. Your current age
2. How many years you plan to continue working for money
3. How much money you have in savings today
4. How much money you plan to save in each future year
5. Whether the amount you save in each future year will increase or decrease (e.g., because you get an annual pay raise or a promotion or because you take time off for travel, health, children, etc.)
6. How much money you plan to spend each year once you have stopped working, in today's dollars
7. How long you expect to live (or how long you want your money to last your family members after you die)
8. The annual inflation rate in the US dollar (or whatever your local currency is)
9. How much money you pay in taxes on the money you withdraw once you stop working
10. The rate of return that you get when you invest your savings

There are retirement calculators online that you can play with. You can input different numbers and model your future financial situation based on various assumptions. As you play with the numbers, it quickly becomes apparent that, of the ten factors, number ten—rate of return—is by far the biggest determinant of your financial success. How much money you earn and save is important, but your rate of return determines the quality of your life.

In short, your rate of return is the amount of money you make plus the period over which you make it. Let's say you invest $100 on January 1, 2018. By December 31, 2018, your investment has gone up to $108—an 8 percent annualized return. Rate of return is generally expressed as an annual number, but it can also be expressed as an absolute number. For example, let's again say that you invest $100 on January 1, 2018. Five years later, on December 31, 2022, your investment is worth $200. Your absolute rate of return is 100 percent because your money has doubled. But your *annualized* rate of return is 15 percent, meaning you made 15 percent each year for five years. The takeaway? If you see an investment that advertises a huge rate of return, ask whether that number is an absolute return or an annualized return. This can be deceptive.

So why is rate of return the most important factor in your retirement? Let's illustrate with an example. Jessica is forty-five. She works as a fashion executive in New York City and makes a great living—$200,000 per year. She loves her work but wants to retire at age sixty-five and travel the world. She saves 20 percent of her income every year and spends $100,000 per year. She has $500,000 in savings today and faces 4 percent inflation over the next fifty years.

Let's say Jessica is terrified of investing and never focuses much on it. She invests her savings in a short-term bond fund and earns 2 percent on her money every year. When she retires at age sixty-five, she'll have over $2.1 million in savings.

This might sound good, but if she continues to earn 2 percent on her money in retirement, she'll run out of money at age seventy-one. Age seventy-one?! This is a woman who did everything right. She had a great job. She saved a large percentage of her income. But a 2 percent rate of return won't get her where she wants to go, especially when inflation is 4 percent. Jessica thought she was investing, but she was losing 2 percent of her money to inflation every year.

Let's look at an alternate situation in which Jessica made different choices. In this version of the story, Jessica invests her savings in an S&P 500 stock index fund. Some years the US stock market is up and some years it's down, but on the whole, Jessica earns 8 percent on her money every year. When she retires at age sixty-five, she'll have over $4.5 million in savings. If she continues to earn 8 percent on her money in retirement, she'll run out of money at age eighty-eight. Eight percent return with 4 percent inflation means that Jessica is earning 4 percent on her money, on an inflation-adjusted basis. This is a more "typical" retirement model and generally reflects the assumptions embedded in software models at big financial planning firms.

Finally, let's take Jessica the superinvestor. She uses the techniques of the world's best hedge fund managers. Some years she does better than others, but, on the whole, Jessica earns 15 percent on her money every year. When Jessica retires at age sixty-five, she'll have almost $11.8 million in savings. If Jessica continues to earn 15 percent on her money in retirement, she'll have $263 million when she's eighty-eight. $263 million?! It can be hard to fathom that a single factor—Jessica's rate of return—makes the difference between financial ruin, financial peace, or astronomical wealth.

Let's take one final, more extreme example. Julie is thirty and has a hugely successful career. She makes $1 million per year as the chief technology officer for a Silicon Valley firm.

She saves about $500,000 per year because, although she loves her work, she knows she doesn't want to run at this pace forever.

Julie should be set for life, right? Here's her picture:

- If she gets a 3 percent rate of return on her savings, she will have to work until the day she dies. This is because inflation likely will eat up every dollar she saves.
- If she gets an 8 percent rate of return, then she is free around age thirty-seven. She can spend about $200,000 per year for the rest of her life without ever working.
- If she gets a 15 percent rate of return, she is free around age thirty-four, and she'll probably be a billionaire by the end of her life.

What are the takeaways from these stories? First, and again, your rate of return determines the quality of your life. A 15 percent rate of return on a reasonable savings percentage gives you astronomical wealth. Certainly, a 15 percent rate of return is not easy to achieve. The best investors and hedge fund managers in the world are thrilled with a 15 percent rate of return. But it's worth looking at the investment strategies those professionals employ to see what we can learn (and copy). We'll do this soon.

Second, retirement is expensive. If you want to retire at age sixty-five, you have to save a lot of money and invest well. If you want to retire at age fifty, you have to save *even more* money and *really* invest well.

As you plan the nuts and bolts of your retirement strategy, it's also worth taking a beat to consider what's really aligned for you when it comes to career and retirement. The irony is that many people retire, spend the first three months organizing their closets and reveling in their newfound freedom, and then struggle with meaning, purpose, and ultimately mental and physical health. Work represents so much more than income: As Neil Pasricha describes in *The Happiness Equation*, it also provides "Social, Structure, Stimulation and Story." Many meaningful relationships are built through work partnerships. Work also provides some structured balance between activity and rest, regardless of whether you have a set schedule or the freedom to manage your own time. It can provide a mental or physical challenge. And it can provide meaning and purpose, especially if you feel your work serves others or has a positive impact in the world.

So it's worth asking whether you are running toward retirement because you're stuck in a job you hate—and if so, what are the alternatives? A good litmus test is the calculator game. If you find yourself sitting at work every day obsessively plugging eighteen different iterations of your retirement numbers into an online retirement calculator, it might be time to co-create a new career. By using the tools in part 1, you can create a working life and an income stream that makes you wonder why anyone would ever want to retire. Certainly, saving at least 10 percent is important, regardless of whether you want retirement tomorrow or never want to retire. But being laser focused on retirement means you might miss the chance to find joy in meaningful, aligned, low-stress work along the way. It's wonderful to have duplicate sources of financial abundance. Not only can you rely on your portfolio of savings and investment, but you can also rely on your ability to make money doing something you love while living a life you love.

CHAPTER 15

Demystify the Investing Lingo

You've likely heard the investing terminology: stocks, bonds, equity, debt, preferred stock, CDs, index funds, hedge funds, private equity funds—and then it all starts to run together. These investment terms describe different ways that you and I, as investors, can give money to companies, governments, and other institutions that need money to fulfill their missions, and have the opportunity to make money for ourselves along the way. Sometimes our investment is direct, like loaning your friend $1,000 to start her new skateboard company. Sometimes our investment is rather indirect, like buying shares of a mutual fund that invests in Eastern European manufacturing companies. But the objective is the same—I, the investor, give money to a business.

Consider this chapter your glossary of investing terms. Feel free to read it straight through or simply come back to it as a reference.

STOCK (A.K.A. EQUITY)

Stock represents ownership in a company. For example, let's say that you and your brother form a company to start a bakery. The company issues one hundred shares of stock. You own fifty shares and your brother owns fifty shares, which means you each own 50 percent of the bakery. Publicly traded companies like Apple, Google, and Amazon work the same way. If Apple has sixteen billion shares of stock outstanding and you buy one hundred shares of Apple, then you own 0.000000625 percent of Apple Inc. Although it feels decidedly less tangible to own a tiny percentage of Apple than it does to own half a local business, your relationship to the company is the same. You own part of the company, and as an owner of the company, you should benefit if the company sells more stuff and makes more money.

BOND (A.K.A. FIXED INCOME OR DEBT)

A bond is a piece of paper (physical or digital) that a company gives you when you lend it money. Again, let's say you and your brother form a company and start a bakery. The company needs $3,000 to buy a new oven. You lend the company $3,000 of cash and, in exchange, the company gives you an IOU. The IOU says that the company promises to pay you $792 every year for the next five years. In other words, the company will not only give your $3,000 back to you, but it will also pay 10 percent interest. You'll receive a total of $3,960 from the company over the next five years, and that extra $960 is just because the company had the privilege of borrowing money from you.

Again, big publicly traded companies like Apple, Google, and Amazon work the same way. If you buy a bond from Apple, you agree to lend the company a certain amount of money for a certain amount of time. In exchange, Apple agrees to pay you principal plus interest at a fixed interval (e.g., every six months). You not only get your money back, but you also get interest payments.

Why would Apple borrow money from you? Because they believe they can make an investment that will generate more return than the interest rate they are paying you. For example, if they can borrow $100 million and build a new factory that will generate $500 million of profit for the next ten years, they don't mind paying $11 million of interest to bondholders every year.

People often say that bonds are a safer, more conservative investment than stock. This is generally true because (a) bonds have payment priority in bankruptcy and (b) interest payments on bonds are generally fixed and do not depend on whether the company has profits or losses. If a company goes bankrupt, bondholders will be repaid first, and stockholders get any left-over money. (Hint: there typically isn't any leftover money in bankruptcy for stockholders.) This is another reason to look for profitable companies and try not to buy stock (or bonds, for that matter) of companies that could potentially go bankrupt.

PREFERRED STOCK

Preferred stock is a bit like a stock-bond hybrid. Preferred stock is great because preferred stockholders (1) are owners of the company, just like common (i.e., normal) stockholders, (2) generally get a higher dividend payout than common stock-holders, and (3) get their money back after bondholders but before common stockholders in the event of bankruptcy. The price of preferred stock also tends to move less than the price of common stock, so you may not have as much of a roller-coaster ride owning preferred stock as you would common stock. The downside to this is that if the company does really well, common stockholders can make a lot of money, whereas preferred stockholders might not make as much money. But preferred stock has its place, especially if the dividend payouts are high.

CERTIFICATES OF DEPOSIT

Certificates of deposit, or CDs, are IOUs from a bank. When you buy a CD from a bank, you are agreeing to let the bank keep your money for a fixed period—usually anywhere from three months to five years. In exchange for the longer period, the bank pays you a bit more interest than it would pay you on a normal savings account. Bank CDs are insured by the Federal Deposit Insurance Corporation (FDIC) and credit union CDs are insured by the National Credit Union Administration (NCUA). This insurance can protect you if the bank you buy the CD from fails.

SECURITIES

Securities is an umbrella term for any financial asset that you can, or could potentially, trade. Stocks are a type of security. Bonds are also a type of security.

SECURITIES EXCHANGE

A securities exchange is a place where you can buy or sell, well, securities. For example, you can buy and sell stocks, bonds, or options (more on options later) on the New York Stock Exchange, the Tokyo Stock Exchange, or the London Stock Exchange.

INDEX

An index is a list of stocks or other securities. This list is compiled by a private company. For example, let's say you and I wanted to make our own index of the one hundred biggest food companies in Mexico. We could call it the MexFood100 Index. Similarly, Standard & Poor's (S&P) is a company that publishes a list of the five hundred largest and most prominent US publicly traded companies. This index is called the S&P 500 Index. There are a lot of indexes in the world— indexes that track Malaysian bonds, Turkish stocks, or lithium-ion battery companies. If you can think of a category or a type of investment, there is probably an index for it.

FUND

A fund is an investment product. A private fund company will create a legal entity that goes out and buys securities. Then, we, as investors, can buy shares in the fund—the legal entity. Our ownership of those fund shares means that we indirectly have exposure to the securities that the fund owns. Funds can be a way to "buy" a lot of different securities without incurring the cost and headache of purchasing each security individually.

Funds come in two primary flavors: exchange-traded funds (ETFs) and mutual funds. One difference is that shares of an ETF are traded on a securities exchange, whereas mutual fund shares are purchased directly through the fund company (e.g., T. Rowe Price). The other difference is that, when you own shares of a mutual fund, you actually own a percentage of the securities that the mutual fund owns. When you own shares of an ETF, you do not actually own any percentage of the underlying assets in the ETF.

If a mutual fund is an orange, then an ETF is orange juice—a slightly more processed financial product. There are more players involved in an ETF, which introduces more systemic risk. But ETFs have two primary benefits: (1) There is generally no minimum investment for an ETF, and (2) you can trade options on many ETFs to generate extra income.

INDEX FUND

An index fund is an easy way to "buy the whole market." Let's say you want to buy all the stocks that are part of the S&P 500 index. One option would be to go out and buy all five hundred stocks yourself. You would buy shares of Boeing, shares of American Express, shares of Biogen, and shares of 497 other companies. If this sounds expensive and extremely inconvenient, it is. Instead, fund companies like Vanguard, State Street, and others offer S&P 500 index mutual funds and S&P 500 ETFs. You buy shares of the mutual fund or ETF, and the fund buys shares of each company in the S&P 500.

The idea is that if the value of the securities inside the fund goes up or down, the value of your ownership interest in the fund also goes up or down. You can get financial returns that mirror the securities in the index without actually owning the underlying securities (stocks, bonds, etc.).

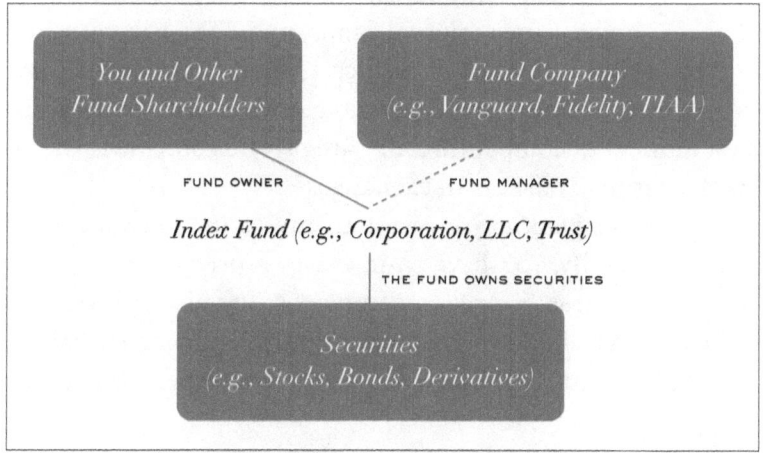

HEDGE FUND

A hedge fund is an exclusive mutual fund with high fees. The fund is "exclusive" because it hasn't jumped through the legal and regulatory hurdles that funds must jump through in order to market and sell their shares to the general public. Instead, hedge funds operate under a limited regulatory exception, which allows the hedge fund to avoid compliance with certain securities laws as long as they only sell fund shares to people and entities that have a certain amount of money. The idea (or perhaps myth) here is that people above a certain wealth threshold should be sophisticated enough to evaluate investment risks for themselves. Some hedge funds simply invest in publicly traded stocks, while other funds use sophisticated options strategies or quantitative models. Hedge funds traditionally charge 2 percent of assets under management, plus 20 percent of any profits on the underlying investments (i.e., they're expensive).

PRIVATE EQUITY FUND

A private equity fund is a fund that invests in private companies. As we've seen, many stocks trade on public securities exchanges. Hedge funds, mutual funds, and ETFs generally buy and sell public securities. But since 1990, the number of companies "going public" on exchanges has dropped, and a significant number of companies today are private companies whose stock does not trade on an exchange.

What happens if you want to invest in a private company? Generally, you have to invest in a private equity fund that owns shares in private companies. Private equity funds typically have high investment minimums and high fees; these funds also require you to show significant assets or income.

However, publicly traded private equity funds can offer a way to invest in private companies. Crowdfunding platforms also attempt to democratize access to private companies.

TICKER SYMBOL

Stocks, ETFs, and mutual funds all have unique identifying codes. For example, the ticker symbol for Apple stock is AAPL and the ticker symbol for Southwest Airlines stock is LUV. When you buy and sell securities, you will enter the ticker symbol into the trade box inside your brokerage account to tell your brokerage firm that you would like to buy or sell the security.

As you become more comfortable placing trades, you'll start to recognize patterns in ticker symbols. For example, mutual funds generally have ticker symbols that are five letters long, and the ticker symbol for a mutual fund always ends with the letter X. The ticker symbol for an ETF is generally three letters. Ticker symbols for individual stocks vary in length from one to five letters.

BASIS POINT

A basis point is one one-hundredth of a percentage point. For example, fifty basis points is one-half of one percent (i.e., 0.5 percent). Seventy-five basis points is three-quarters of one percent (i.e., 0.75 percent).

Basis points often come up when you listen to news about the US Federal Reserve. For example, you might hear "The Federal Reserve raised the federal funds rate by twenty-five basis points today," which means the target interest rate went up by 0.25 percent.

STOCK OPTIONS

Stock options are insurance policies, but for securities.

There are two types of options: call options and put options. A call option is a contract that gives someone the right to buy a security for a set price for a certain period. A put option is a contract that gives someone the right to sell a security for a set price for a certain period. You can buy or sell a call option. You can also buy or sell a put option.

Confused? Let's walk through two examples.

Example 1: Let's say your sister bought Disney stock for $100, and her investment is now worth $180. Your sister doesn't want to lose money on her investment, and she is afraid that Disney stock will drop below $100 per share, where she bought it. So she buys a put option from you for $25 of premium. If her Disney stock drops below $100, she has the right to sell the stock to you for $100, even though it's only worth, say, $70 now that the market has tanked. You are stuck paying $100 for something that is only worth $70 right now.

Why would your sister buy a put option? In this example, your sister pays good money for a put option because she has insurance against a big market drop. You sell her the insurance because you get $25 cash up front. But, most importantly, you sell her the insurance because you want to buy Disney at $100 per share anyway. If you aren't willing to buy Disney at $100 per share, then you have no business selling put options because you never know when the market will tank and you will have to make good on your promise to buy Disney. In other words, selling a put option lets you get extra cash to do what you were going to do anyway. But we never sell a put option just to gamble on the fact that it won't actually be put to us.

Example 2: Let's look at a call option. Again, assume your sister bought Disney stock for $100, and her investment is now worth $180. Your sister would be willing to sell her Disney stock for $200 because she thinks that Disney stock isn't worth much more than that. So she sells you a call option for $30 of premium. If her Disney stock appreciates to, say, $240, then you can buy the stock from her for $200, even though it's now worth $240. If the market jumps dramatically, you get the right to buy something for less than it's currently worth, which feels good.

Why would your sister sell a call option? In this example, your sister gets $30 of cash to do what she would have done anyway. She wanted to sell Disney stock once it hit $200, and she generated extra cash flow by selling you the call option. You buy the insurance because you think Disney is worth more than $200, and you want the right to buy it for a favorable price. Importantly, your sister should only sell a call option if she (a) already owns Disney stock and (b) is willing to part with her stock for $200.

In sum, the options market works because people have very different views about what a particular stock or security is worth.

Note: The example about your sister is just to illustrate the point. In real life, options trade on securities exchanges, so you don't necessarily know who your counterparty is.

CONCLUSION

The financial services industry loves to complicate things. If there is a financial term you don't understand, the problem is not you. The problem is the explanation. You deserve an explanation that is clear, in plain English, and easy to understand. You deserve to have your questions answered. And perhaps most importantly, we never, ever invest in things we don't understand, because we don't have time for convoluted complexity.

CHAPTER 16

Dial In Your Asset Allocation

Asset allocation is the pie chart of your investments. It defines how you divvy up your money. For example, let's say you have $10,000 of cash sitting in your Roth IRA. And you're looking at it and wondering, "What's the best way to invest this money?" You understand intuitively that it's probably not a good idea to put the full $10,000 into one single investment; diversification, or "Don't put all your eggs in one basket," is an important way to manage the risk that any one investment may go south. Specifically, when it comes to asset allocation and healthy diversification, there are two relevant questions:

1. How much money should I invest in any given investment? If I decide that I want to invest in, say, the Coca-Cola Company, how much money should I invest? For example, if my total portfolio is $10,000, should I invest one percent (i.e., $100)

in Coca-Cola? Ten percent (i.e., $1,000) in Coca-
Cola? What is an appropriate position size for any
given investment?

2. How should I allocate my money among different asset classes? Here, *asset class* simply means
a category of investment. Stocks are an asset
class. Bonds are an asset class. Commodities are
an asset class. So, for example, you might ask,
"Should I put 60 percent in stocks and 40 percent
in bonds? Fifty percent in bonds and 50 percent in
commodities?" And so on.

The answer to the first question—how much to put in any
given investment—depends on the riskiness of the investment.
I rarely invest more than three percent of my portfolio in an
individual stock. But I might invest a larger percentage in a
diversified bond fund because the price of a bond fund historically has tended to be less volatile.

The answer to the second question—how I should allocate
among different asset classes—hinges on the current economic
environment. An economic environment is made up of two
components. The first component is economic growth. (*Gross
domestic product*, or *GDP*, is often used as shorthand for *economic growth*.) The second component is inflation. Inflation
is a double-edged sword because it tends to raise the price of
everything—not only the goods and services that we purchase
every day (e.g., groceries, gas, etc.) but also the price of stocks,
real estate, and other investments that we might own. Putting
economic growth and inflation together, we get a matrix. In
any given country, at any given time, there are four possible
economic environments. We can have inflation or deflation in
the local currency, and these can be combined with growing
economic activity or declining economic activity (a.k.a. recession). In other words, at any given time in any given country,

we can have (1) inflation combined with economic growth, (2) inflation combined with economic decline (a.k.a. stagflation), (3) deflation combined with economic growth, or (4) deflation combined with economic decline.

Once we have determined the economic environment, we look at which assets tend to perform well in that environment. Historically, cash has tended to shine when there is deflation combined with an economic recession. In other words, when the economy is tending toward depression, cash is our friend. Gold has tended to shine when there is inflation or hyperinflation combined with an economic recession. This makes sense because psychologically, gold is a safe-haven asset that tends to go up when cash is losing its value. Stocks have tended to shine when there is inflation combined with economic growth; in other words, when things are growing, stocks tend to increase in value. And finally, bonds have tended to shine when there is deflation combined with economic growth. This is especially true for corporate bonds. In contrast, US government bonds tend to be less sensitive to whether the US economy is growing or shrinking. This is because they (at least historically) derive a lot of their value from the fact that the US is the world's global reserve currency, and less value from the year-to-year fluctuations in the performance of the US economy.

Putting this together, we can adjust our asset allocation to reflect not only the riskiness of the individual investment, but also the current economic environment. For example, we might allocate more to gold and less to stocks when the economy is shrinking. Although it does require a bit more work on our part to keep tabs on the current economic environment and the changing winds, this monitoring and adjustment process is not a daily or weekly exercise. It is something we can do a few times per year, and it helps ensure that our investment mix is appropriate for the times.

CHAPTER 17

Invest Well

As people, we invest in so many things. We invest in our relationships, our children, our education, our careers, our
health, and our communities. We use our money to make
nonprofit donations, take personal growth classes, and care
for our children. But when it comes to our portfolios—the 10
percent of gross income that we save and invest—we need to
have strong energetic boundaries around what investing is and
what it isn't. These strong energetic boundaries give us the best
chance of investing success. The goal here is to make money
on our money, and that is a very specific endeavor.

WHAT INVESTING IS

This is investing in its most basic sense: (1) I give a business
money, (2) that business does something profitable with my

money, and (3) that business gives me back more money than I invested. For example, let's say you and I each invest $100,000 in an LLC to support a local permaculture farm (i.e., $200,000 of total capital invested). That LLC goes out and buys ten acres of agricultural land. The LLC hires a farmer who works the land and manages the farm. The LLC also buys supplies and equipment—seeds, trees, tractors, irrigation equipment, etc. The LLC pays property taxes and water bills and insurance costs.

The first year, the permaculture operation doesn't make any money because the plants are still growing. But starting in year two and each year thereafter, the permaculture farm produces and sells $150,000 of product to customers. The LLC keeps $130,000 to pay the farmer, pay all the farm's expenses, and to keep some capital on hand to replace aging equipment and also to one day expand the farm. (The LLC hopes to buy additional acreage and introduce a new line of branded products in the next few years.)

The LLC distributes $10,000 to you and $10,000 to me every year. That means that we each enjoy a 10 percent annual rate of return on our invested capital (i.e., $10,000 ÷ $100,000 = 10 percent every year). Our investment turns out to be a wonderful investment, thanks to a wonderfully run permaculture operation. The farmer, the equipment, the customers, Mother Nature, and a bit of good fortune all swirl together to create something that is more valuable and more profitable than each part standing alone. It feels like business alchemy.

Business alchemy can apply in all sorts of fields. For example, in technology, alchemy could mean that the right team of software engineers comes together to develop groundbreaking code. That software company might not need much in the way of "stuff"—some leased office space and a big snack drawer will suffice. In contrast, a luxury car maker might find business alchemy by producing beautiful cars efficiently (i.e., at low cost) and branding and marketing the cars such that consumers gladly pay a premium price for a luxury vehicle.

As investors, our job is not to create business alchemy. Instead, we leave the alchemy to the business's management team. Our role is to identify profitable businesses and invest our money in them.

WHAT INVESTING ISN'T

Our definition of investing—(1) I give a business money, (2) that business does something profitable with my money, and (3) that business gives me back more money than I invested— may seem comically simple. And it is. But this definition protects you against three major investing pitfalls: (1) Investing in something that seems like the wave of the future (but that isn't profitable), (2) investing in something merely in the hope that it will go up (but that isn't profitable), and (3) investing in a good cause (that isn't profitable).

Investing in the Wave of the Future

Let's say it's 1945, and you just got a big postwar bonus at work. You add 10 percent of your bonus to your long-term portfolio and start looking for a good investment. You see the writing on the wall—television is going to be the next big thing. And you're exactly right. In 1942, there were about five thousand televisions in America. About ten years later, that number was closer to twenty million. That is astronomical market growth by any measure.

Fortunately, you acted on your brilliant thesis and bought ten shares of the United States Television Manufacturing Corporation for three dollars per share in early 1946 when it went public (i.e., you invested thirty dollars, which was a significant sum back then). The company seemed to be doing well. It was giving well-publicized product demonstrations at big department stores like Bloomingdale's and Macy's in Manhattan. It started producing several new models to complement its original TV set. And by 1950, the company was . . . out of business. Gone. And you lost most if not all of your thirty-dollar investment. How did this happen? The company was in the right industry, but it was poorly managed. If you had purchased stock in another well-known TV company in 1945, like General Electric, you would have had a much stronger outcome.

The point is that it's not enough to be right about the next hot industry. Sure, electric autonomous vehicles, drones, flying cars, 3D printing, solar power, hydrogen power, quantum computing, artificial intelligence, blockchain, and vertical farming could be good places to look for exponential growth. But we also have to find companies inside those industries that are well managed and profitable. In fact, some of the best investors in the world focus on well-managed companies in boring, established industries. As a rule of thumb, focus on company selection first and industry consideration second.

Investing in Something Merely in the Hope That It Will Go Up

Energetically, investing on the hope that something will appreciate feels very much like investing in the wave of the future. Analytically, these two concepts are related but distinct. Investing in the wave of the future means you're investing in a trendy industry, but it could also mean that you're investing in an ungrounded, unprofitable, poorly managed company. Investing in something merely in the hope that it will appreciate often means you're not investing in a company at all.

Cryptocurrency is a good example. Also known as *crypto*,

cryptocurrency is the generic term for digital money that is tied to a blockchain. A blockchain uses encryption to create a record of all the transactions that have happened on the blockchain. For example, on the Bitcoin blockchain, if your brother pays you one Bitcoin, then that transaction is permanently recorded on the blockchain. Your brother cannot turn around and pay that same one Bitcoin to your sister because the Bitcoin network would reject the transaction as fraudulent or "double spending." People say cryptocurrency is a money revolution because it allows two strangers to transact directly, without a middleman, in the digital realm. Without cryptocurrency, two strangers can meet in person and exchange physical cash, but any digital or electronic money transfer must go through a network controlled by a company or affiliated with a bank or government (e.g., Visa, ACH, Swift, etc.).

Certainly, you can make money on Bitcoin if you buy it and the price goes up. But Bitcoin itself is not an enterprise that generates profits or additional value. Compare that to, say, a cryptocurrency company like Coinbase that runs an exchange and that can generate profits by charging fees to customers.

Raw commodities are another example. Commodities include things like metals (e.g., gold, silver, platinum, etc.), energy (e.g., oil, coal, natural gas, etc.), and agriculture (e.g., coffee, corn, wheat, etc.). Certainly, you can make money investing in commodities if you buy the commodity and the price goes up (investors typically use commodities futures contracts to bet on the price of a commodity without actually owning the commodity—trading an oil contract is a lot easier than storing a barrel of oil in your basement!).

However, market forces outside our control (and my depth of understanding) typically drive the market price of a commodity. These forces include global supply and demand, geopolitics, weather, and government policy. Certainly, there are commodity producers that can generate profit over and above the dictated market price for their commodity. For example, a farmer who markets and packages her own herbal teas can generate profits above and beyond the cost of the raw herbs. A gold miner who has her own jewelry line could generate additional profits. But, as a general rule, trying to anticipate changes in the price of lithium, nickel, coffee, or oil feels more like speculating than investing because it is such a complex global puzzle.

Investing in a Good Cause

There are plenty of opportunities to "invest" in nonprofit organizations or make below-market loans. Many nonprofits do wonderful work, and I absolutely encourage you to donate generously to causes you care about, if that aligns with your authenticity. You can also make below-market loans, zero-interest loans, or outright gifts to people who can't otherwise access capital or who could use a leg up. This might be a microloan to an entrepreneur in a developing country, a zero-interest loan to a small organic farmer who is just starting out, or a cash gift to your neighbor who is going through a hard time.

However, we must distinguish between donation and investment. A charitable donation is not an investment because you do not get a financial return on your money, even if the charity thanks you for "investing" in their mission. Below-market loans and zero-interest loans are not investments because you do not get an adequate financial return on your money (i.e., for the capital you are tying up). By all means, if you want to be charitable, be charitable. If you want to invest your money, invest your money. But do not conflate these two concepts.

INVESTMENT SELECTION

To drill down a bit, the following is the four-part framework I use to analyze a business before investing. My core philosophy is not that I'm buying stocks or bonds; rather, I'm buying a business. Certainly, in most cases, I'm only buying a small portion of it because I'm buying a small percentage of the stock. But my mindset is that of a business owner—I analyze the company as if I'm going to buy the whole thing. If I'm not willing to own all of XYZ company, then I have no business owning XYZ stock.

Part 1: Good Impact

Here, the question is, Is this business having a positive impact on the world? As an investor, I get to vote my personal values—and I don't like to compromise on my values. Coal companies may be making money hand over fist, but unless I'm convinced that they are aggressively transitioning to alternative energies, I don't want to invest in them. That's my personal value judgment.

This is where our personal, authentic value systems from chapter 1 come in. You may love coal companies and view them as the engine that has powered an extraordinary era of economic development and human progress. You wouldn't be wrong, and an investment in a coal company could be a beautiful reflection of your personal ethos. The point is, you should only invest in companies that are having a positive impact on the world, however you define positive impact.

The second consideration here: Can I understand this business? I never invest in things I don't understand, for two reasons. First, there are too many wonderful businesses in the world that I *can* understand, so there's no need to waste my time and money on businesses that I can't understand. Second, it's far too easy for a company to obscure shady behavior behind complexity—think the third tranche of a commercial mortgage-backed security that helped cause the financial crash of 2008. Or, at the very least, complexity can hold a business back and slow its growth. That quantum computing drone-based healthcare cooperative for doulas may be the next big thing. But it's beyond my ability and desire to comprehend, so I'm going to take a pass.

Part 2: Good People

Businesses are a collection of people working together, so this is where I consider the people involved and how well they collaborate. This means exploring certain questions:

1. Do I trust leadership (i.e., CEO and key executives) to behave with integrity? To be honest, balanced, and forthright? (The tone of the shareholder letter and videos, media, and shareholder conference call appearances all offer great opportunities to feel out leadership.)
2. Is leadership overpaid?
3. Is leadership buying or selling stock in the company? (The SEC requires companies to disclose certain insider trades.)
4. How happy are the employees? (Social media plus sites like Glassdoor can provide key insights.)

The motivation here is twofold. Certainly, we don't want to support unethical behavior. For example, unhappy employees might suggest labor abuses. And there are potential financial pitfalls. Overpaid leadership means less money for employees and for us as investors. Unethical leadership means there is potential for accounting fraud or legal trouble. And if insiders are dumping their stock as quickly as they can, it's quite possible that the company is experiencing financial problems that haven't come to public light yet, which we as investors would want to avoid.

Part 3: Good Profit

Once I have a good sense for the company, I analyze the numbers by diving into their financial statements. I read the annual report (the Form 10-K) thoroughly. My key metrics:

1. How much debt does this company have relative to the amount of bottom-line profit it brings in every year? I generally want this ratio to be less than three. For example, if a company has $1,000 of debt and it only makes $100 of net profit every year, it would take the company ten years to cover its debt. That's a pass for me. If the company had $300 of debt and it was making $100 of net profit every year, that's a green light to keep analyzing.

2. How hard is it to compete with this company? What is its competitive advantage? Could I compete with this company if someone gave me $1 billion? If the answer is yes—it would be easy to compete with the company—then I take a pass. I want the company to be dominant in its industry.

3. Has the company grown steadily over the last ten years? Certainly, past performance doesn't guarantee future success. But I want to understand the company's track record so that I can make an educated guess about its future. Specifically, to measure growth, I look at four numbers:

- Growth in the company's net profit (i.e., its bottom line)
- Growth in the company's book value (i.e., the
value of all the company's assets if it were to close
tomorrow, pay off its debts, and sell all its assets)
- Growth in the company's revenue (i.e., how
much money the company earns every year before it pays any of its expenses)
- Growth in the company's operating cash (i.e.,
actual cash the company brings in the door, not
just its "revenue" as reported under the accounting rules)

4. What are the company's plans for future growth?
   Will its growth peak within the next few years
   and then fizzle out? Or would I want to own this
   company for at least ten years?
5. How well does the company use investor money?
   To get an idea, I look at both the company's
   return on equity (ROE) and the company's return
   on invested capital (ROIC). ROE is defined as
   the company's net income divided by its equity,
   which is reported on the balance sheet, and it is a
   good indicator of how well the company is using
   investor money. However, a company can arti-
   ficially boost its ROE number by taking on debt
   because debt can boost net income. So I look at
   ROIC as well because ROIC accounts for debt, not
   just equity. The formula for ROIC is net income
   divided by debt *plus* equity. I want both the ROE
   and the ROIC numbers to be healthy over the last
   ten years, which tells me that the company consistently uses investor money well without taking
   on excessive debt.

6. Does this company have enough cash on hand to survive for several years if unforeseen calamity or recession strikes? How did this company perform during the last recession?

Part 4: Good Price

The best risk management advice I have is to buy a company when it's on sale. I carefully look at the business from a qualitative and quantitative perspective and evaluate its leadership. But I also know that it's extremely difficult to predict the future, and that my best analysis invariably will be wrong. So if I have been lucky enough to find a wonderful company that I would like to own, I start the valuation process.

First, I calculate what I think a share of the company is worth today. I use three different valuation methods and take the highest of the three numbers, but all three methods are based on the company's historical profitability and my best assessment of how quickly profits will grow in the future. Next, I slash my valuation in half, and that is the price at which I'm willing to buy shares of a company. For example, if I calculate that shares of Sprouts Farmers Market are worth fifty dollars per share, the most I'll pay for one share of Sprouts is twenty-five dollars.

The idea here is that my valuation is inherently going to be wrong. Any valuation model depends on assumptions about the future, which means the number that the valuation model spits out is just an educated guess. Cutting my valuation in half gives me plenty of room for error. Even if my educated guess is pretty far off, my target buy price is extremely conservative, so it can compensate for a lot of bad guessing. In other words, even if I'm very wrong about how profitable the company will be in the future, I want to put myself in a position to not lose money on the investment. Sale shopping for investments is the most effective risk management tool I've found.

SO, DOES INVESTING MAKE ME
A DIRTY CAPITALIST?

Technically, yes.

When it comes to investing your money—your personal financial capital—you want to find profitable companies and you want those companies to return profits to you as the investor (i.e., the shareholder who owns the company or the bondholder who owns the company's debt). And, to exaggerate the point, strictly speaking, as investors, we really only care about two things: (1) how much profit our company is making and (2) how much of that profit is coming back into our pockets. We don't care whether the company is exploiting workers, destroying the environment, or screwing customers.

Except that there's more to the story.

First, we don't invest in a vacuum. Even if we were cold and heartless capitalists, the world is of course interconnected—increasingly so. We are all waking up to the fact that myopic exploitation of Mother Earth and our fellow humans simply isn't sustainable.

Second, capitalism is so much more than investing in stocks and bonds. *Merriam-Webster* defines *capitalism* as "an economic system characterized by private or corporate ownership of capital goods, by investments that are determined by private decision, and by prices, production, and the distribution of goods that are determined mainly by competition in a free market."[1] In other words, capitalism is a system. And the zeitgeist often equates capitalism with income inequality, economic oppression, racial oppression, social injustice, corrupt politicians, dysfunctional government, bad public policy, gridlock, broken systems, environmental destruction, pollution, climate change, shadow, and darkness.

---

1.   "capitalism." Merriam-Webster.com. 2024. https://www.merriam
     -webster.com.

And those are undeniable realities in our world today. But let's not throw the baby out with the bathwater. We can invest our savings in the stocks and bonds of profitable companies without becoming evil capitalists or feeding antiquated, inequitable systems.

If we believe fundamentally that money and investing are inherently dark, we have a mental block that needs to be addressed. This "money is evil" worldview means we'll spend our lives pouting on the sidelines rather than getting in the game and being a positive light in the world, financially and otherwise.

Ultimately, good investors get really basic. They tune out the vast majority of news—news about the world-altering trend du jour, the hottest new stock, the geopolitical collapse, and the impending economic whatever. Sure, they hear it all. But they know that 99.9 percent of the time, this news doesn't change their investment strategy.

As a successful long-term investor, you may, say, find yourself at a cocktail party one day. Some man will be talking about his latest and greatest investment. He'll tell you that he bought X for $100 and sold it for $100,000. And, because you're human, you will feel a knot in the pit of your stomach. You'll feel like you're missing out. You'll feel like you're doing it wrong. You'll question your investment strategy and doubt your portfolio. And that's okay. As an investor, you will feel the full spectrum of emotions—fear, doubt, anxiety, joy, pride, and more. But the most important lesson from this chapter is to *stay grounded*. When we feel triggered or activated, we can always ground back in our comically simple definition of investing: (1) I give a business money, (2) that business does something profitable with my money, and (3) that business gives me back more money than I invested. If you can get these three things to line up, you'll have more money than you'll ever need.

Putting It All Together

Part 1 explored the art of co-creating a career and income stream that you love. Part 2 explored different types of accounts. And part 3 explored the art of investing well. How do all these pieces fit together? Let's tour through some narratives.

CASE STUDY I

Meg is in her late thirties. She is in the process of divorcing her husband of nearly fifteen years. She has two daughters in elementary school and lives outside Dallas, Texas. She works as an HR manager for a midsize company and makes good money. She feels ashamed and embarrassed that she knows so little about money and finance—she's a mother of two daughters and has a master's degree! But her soon-to-be ex-husband is an accountant and has always handled the money.

Meg isn't calling in a career change or promotion right now. She's happy with her income and certainly doesn't need another major life change on top of her divorce.

She and her husband have a joint checking account. She has a Roth 401(k) plan at work but has historically only contributed the minimum amount necessary to get the employer match. Her husband also has a Roth 401(k) through his job.

She and her husband own their home and have a thirty-year fixed-rate mortgage with a pretty low interest rate. Meg wants to stay in the home and is hopeful that she will get the house in the divorce, along with a monthly payment from her husband to help cover the mortgage. But it's possible that Meg and her husband will need to sell the house and each move in to less expensive housing.

Looking to get her finances in order, Meg develops an action plan:

- She opens an individual checking account in her name alone and starts depositing her paycheck there. (She first checks with her divorce lawyer to make sure it's okay to start segregating assets.)
- She also opens a brokerage account in her name alone and she titles it "Housing." Because she's not sure how the house will shake out in her divorce, she wants to be sure that she could make the security deposit and first few months' rent on an apartment she loves if she and her husband do have to sell their home. It's a conservative move, but it gives her some piece of mind. She invests this money in a money market mutual fund. It doesn't earn a lot of interest, but it's also a very low-risk investment.
- She jots down her expenses and looks to see whether there's anything that's not in alignment. She'd like to increase the amount of money going into her Roth 401(k) plan every year, now that she can't rely on her husband to help fund her retirement.
- She considers whether to open two 529 plan accounts for her daughters. But right now, she's not sure whether she'll be able to help her daughters

with their college expenses. So rather than locking the money up in a dedicated education account, she makes a mental note to revisit the college-savings question down the line. She also tells her divorce lawyer that, if possible, her divorce agreement should say that her husband will help pay for their daughters' college educations, should they decide to go to college.

- On the healthcare front, Meg has the option to contribute to an HSA account at work, but she decides to skip it. She and her family are generally in good health, and she has enough money in her checking account to cover the deductible and co-insurance on her health insurance plan in case of an unexpected medical emergency. She'd rather prioritize retirement savings via her Roth 401(k) contributions right now.

- Finally, Meg takes a close look at the investments inside her Roth 401(k). Her firm only offers a limited menu of ETFs, and Meg would like to diversify into different asset classes and maybe some individual stocks. She calls Fidelity, her firm's 401(k) plan administrator, and asks whether she can do an in-service distribution to roll the money into a Roth IRA while she is still working for her company. She also asks whether there is a way to access a broader range of investment options at Fidelity without having to do an in-service distribution to a Roth IRA.

Fast-forward about a year. Meg has finalized her divorce, found a townhome she loves, and finally feels like she's getting her feet under her. Then, suddenly, the hits start coming. First, her ex-husband sues to change their custody arrangement, saying that their daughters are suffering "mental anguish" because of Meg. She wants to write it off as her ex-husband just being difficult and vindictive. But then, her colleague blames her for deleting all the files off the shared drive at work, something she knows was definitely an IT failure, not a mistake on her part. Her whole department is mad at her, and her boss puts a formal warning in her file, even though she never touched any files. She's terrified that she's going to lose her job. And then, three weeks later, she gets a letter from her landlord. He's saying that she owes $3,500 for ruining the grass and the landscaping outside the townhome. But she's taken meticulous care of the property, and it looks better than it ever has. Meg is totally perplexed. And, finally, it dawns on her: there's a pattern. She has a subconscious loop that says, *"I am the problem!"*

Somewhat heartbreakingly, it's not hard to see where it comes from. Ever since Meg was a little girl, she can remember her mom and dad having violent shouting matches, always about her. They would scream and fight about which sports Meg should play, how Meg should be raised, whether Meg was doing well in school. They thought she couldn't hear them, but she remembers standing on the landing of the stairs late at night, peering down into the living room while her parents argued. Of course, adult Meg understands rationally that her parents had their own individual unresolved issues that simply came out sideways and that it really had nothing to do with her. But precious little five-year-old Meg imprinted her parents' arguments as "I am the problem." And here it is—this pattern is expressing itself in Meg's love life, career, and home.

Committed to healing her wounds and taking control of her own destiny, Meg finds a local EMDR therapist to help her address this pattern. She also adds some guided inner-child meditations from To Be Magnetic, three times a week, to reinforce the EMDR work she's doing. She sticks with it, even though she's not seeing immediate results. And, gradually, she starts to feel more peace and confidence. She finds that it's easier to speak her mind in meetings at work, whereas before she remained relatively quiet. Then, after nine months of legal battle, her ex-husband decides to drop the custody suit out of the blue, saying that he's happy with their current arrangement. And a year after she started the EMDR, she applies for a promotion at work and gets the job! Her boss says he really values her contributions and insights and feels like she's ready for a leadership role. She gets an $18,000 annual raise and uses that money to fund her daughters' college savings accounts.

CASE STUDY 2

Dave is in his mid-forties. He is a physician, and he lives outside New York City with his wife, Julia, and two teenage kids. Julia has a part-time job, but Dave is the primary breadwinner. He has substantial school debt that has a relatively high interest rate. Despite that, he and Julia are both savers, and they have accumulated a significant amount of money in Dave's Roth 401(k) and in a taxable brokerage account. Unfortunately, Dave has increasingly been feeling trapped in his job. He has a long commute and feels like he spends more time dealing with paperwork than making a difference for his patients. On the investing front, Dave and Julia know little. But Julia has gotten curious and is researching options on what to do with their family's money; she and Dave both want to invest in things that are meaningful to them.

Looking to make some changes, Dave and Julia do the following:

- They each open a Roth IRA account and make annual backdoor Roth IRA contributions. They

had been putting extra savings in their brokerage
account but didn't realize that they could contribute both to Dave's Roth 401(k) at work and to
individual Roth IRAs.

- Julia looks at the investment options inside their
  Roth IRAs as well as inside Dave's Roth 401(k)
  account. Dave's medical practice has very few
  restrictions on the investment options inside the
  401(k) plan, so Julia starts taking a more active
  approach to investing their retirement savings,
  changing the asset allocation as the economy
  changes and buying individual stocks of companies that align with their family's values.

- Julia also decides that she wants to manage an
  investment property. She loves interior design and
  has a gift for creating spaces where people love to
  spend time. She takes a bit of money out of their
  brokerage account, gets a thirty-year fixed-rate
  loan with a great interest rate, and makes the
  downpayment on a condo in Brooklyn. She rents
  it out on a short-term basis to people visiting New
  York and gets a 10 percent rate of return in the
  first year.

- Dave has always dreamed of starting his own
  holistic concierge internal medicine practice. A
  few years ago, he decided to see some patients on
  the side to test the waters. He loved the patient
  interaction and having the autonomy to practice
  in a way he felt was best for his patients. But when
  it came time to collect payment, Dave had issues.
  Several patients simply ignored his bills. When he
  tried to call them, they were nowhere to be found.
  Dave concluded that starting his own practice

was simply too risky—he had a family to support. But, in the back of his mind, the dream of entrepreneurship has continued to nag him.

In fact, Dave has some strong patterning around scams and scam artists. It seems like his credit card number is stolen every few months. It's no big deal—the credit card company just sends him a new card with a new number. But it's a pattern. He has been pickpocketed on the train several times over the last few years, even though pickpockets are rare on the train line he takes. And recently, he and Julia hired an estate planning lawyer to help them draft a will and trust. They paid a $5,000 retainer, only to find out that the lawyer wasn't licensed. He was arrested for fraud and unauthorized practice of law shortly after Dave and Julia paid their retainer, but the $5,000 was gone.

It hits Dave like a ton of bricks: "I am the common denominator." Something was looping in Dave's subconscious that said, "You can take advantage of me." It wasn't hard to see the root. When Dave was ten, his parents divorced. His mom was working full-time, so he spent a lot of time with his aunt. She, unbeknownst to Dave's mom, sexually abused him on a regular basis. Horrible, disgusting, and inexcusable. And sweet, defenseless little Dave imprinted, "I deserve to be taken advantage of." Which of course couldn't be further from the truth. No human deserves to be taken advantage of, least of all a child. (As an additional note, the imprints from certain events can and will vary by individual. This is just an example, and it's certainly not to say that sexual abuse or other kinds of abuse necessarily imprint an openness to being taken advantage of. There can be a wide range of imprints, depending on the circumstances. A good therapist can be invaluable in helping to determine a pattern's root issue, if it's not apparent.)

Dave starts his healing journey. He does a training in Transcendental Meditation and practices twenty minutes, twice a day, every day, to help calm and regulate his nervous system. He does a weeklong intensive inner-child boot camp where he learns some healing tools and techniques. Finally, several months after his boot camp, he feels called to try psychedelic-assisted therapy with a licensed, trusted practitioner in his neighborhood.

Although the results aren't immediate, Dave starts to notice some shifts. Eighteen months go by, and his credit card hasn't been stolen once. Dave goes to renew his passport online and ends up on a fake website trying to steal his identity. But he pauses and realizes that this is a test—will he fall for the scam? Dave closes the website and renews his passport directly with the Department of State. At work, one of Dave's colleagues starts trying to pawn problem patients off on Dave. It's yet another test. Will Dave allow himself to be taken advantage of? He politely declines. Finally, Dave gets a series of emails asking him to wire money to a Nigerian prince immediately. He laughs. He knows that the universe has a great sense of humor. When it starts sending you tests that feel like softballs, you know you're close to putting the subconscious issue behind you once and for all.

Dave decides that he's ready to revisit the concept of starting his own practice. He starts to see a few patients on the side, and to his delight, he not only loves working with them but they all pay their bills on time. Dave moves to part time at his day job and eventually transitions to full-time concierge medicine. He earns the same income he did working full-time in the city, but with a much better quality of life. He enjoys no commute, more autonomy, a more meaningful impact for patients, and more time with Julia and their kids—all things that are authentic to Dave.

CASE STUDY 3

Caley is in her early thirties. She lives in the Bay Area and is single. She works as a software engineer and has been getting most of her financial advice from family and friends. As soon as she finishes paying off her student loans, she wants to do some basic investing and save for her own condo or townhome. She really likes the idea of having something she can own and knowing that her housing situation will be stable. She is motivated to up-level her finances and lifestyle and would love to get a second home that gets her closer to nature—maybe in the countryside or the mountains.

Looking to get her finances in order, Caley takes a few steps:

- She realizes during open enrollment season at work that her employer offers a 401(k) match. Caley's student loans have an interest rate of nearly 9 percent, so she has been prioritizing paying those off. But she also doesn't want to leave free money on the table. So Caley opens a Roth 401(k) through her employer and tells her employer to contribute 3 percent of each paycheck to her Roth 401(k) via automatic payroll deduction.
- Caley also knows she is going to need hip replacement surgery to correct her hip dysplasia at some point. It's not urgent, but she knows it will need to be done. So she sets up an HSA through work. Her employer contributes some money every pay period, and Caley contributes the balance so that she maxes out her HSA in 2025 (i.e., the full IRS limit of $4,300 goes into her HSA in 2025).
- Separate from her accounts through work, Caley decides to open a Roth IRA to start saving for the

down payment on her first home. She isn't able to contribute much right now, but it helps her mentally to know that she is earmarking an account for her home-buying goal.

• Caley decides not to open a separate brokerage account to earmark savings for her second home. The second home is a bit of a distant dream right now.

Big picture, Caley is generally happy to have a stable job in a growing field. But these home purchases are important to her. She knows that if she wants to pay off her student debt, save a significant amount for retirement, and save for her first home all at the same time, she's going to need to earn more money. Growing up, Caley's parents both worked good jobs and made good money. But Caley's mom was a hoarder. She held on to everything. She thrifted incessantly, never one to pass up a "good deal." Their house was stacked wall to wall with stuff. From a young age, Caley imprinted, *"There's never enough!"*

Determined to make some changes, Caley does a Transcendental Meditation training. She also starts doing the guided inner-child meditations from To Be Magnetic several times a week. She discovers that the years from zero to eighteen months is a critical developmental window because this is when we learn whether we can trust that our needs will be met or not. If our caretakers are not present and are not able to provide for both our physical and emotional needs, we can imprint a lack mentality at an early age.

Caley sticks with her meditation routine, even though she's not sure whether it's making a difference or not. She also makes some deliberate changes in her purchasing habits. Typically, she only ever purchases something if it is dramatically on sale (think 40 or 50 percent off). But there is a mattress that she has been eyeing for several years. She loves it and knows it would help her sleep, but it never goes on sale. As painful as it is for her to do, she buys the mattress at full price. She also starts trying to focus more on quality over quantity. She decides to bite the bullet and clean out her closet—dozens of jackets, shoes, and pants that she bought on sale but never really loved or wore. She pares down her wardrobe and buys a few key pieces that she loves and uses regularly. It's not easy, especially at first. But Caley finds that it does get easier over time, almost as though she can feel the guided meditations creating new neural networks in her brain.

Fast-forward two years, and Caley opens her email. Her company has announced that they are proactively closing the gender pay gap. They've reviewed salaries across all departments and are taking steps to equalize pay. Later that day, Caley's boss tells her that she has been dramatically underpaid and is getting a $19,000 annual raise—enough to make a significant dent in her home-savings goals. Caley smiles as she realizes that sometimes there actually is enough.

CLOSING THOUGHTS

Saving is important. Organization is important. Tax-advantaged accounts and good investment returns are of course incredibly important. The numbers matter. But the missing piece in personal finance is co-creating the life of your dreams. The goal is not to slog away at a job that you hate for three, four, or even five decades, only to pay for "retirement." The idea shouldn't be that life, joy, connection, and contribution are put on hold until age sixty-five, when you finally have the freedom and space to pursue what is meaningful to you. Instead, let's flip this model on its head.

By honoring the co-creative process—uncovering authenticity, transforming limiting beliefs, contributing in the way that only we can, and clearing space—we can not only craft the life of our dreams but also generate the income and assets we need to fund that dream life. In other words, if we learn how to co-create with the universe, we will be able to set ourselves up for the abundance the universe has to offer us.

Conclusion

Money is not an end in and of itself. Money isn't even a means to an end. Money is energy, and the more you can find flow in your own life, the more money flows in. But too often, statements like "finding flow" or "raising your vibration" are hopelessly abstract, frustratingly unhelpful, and downright misguided. Instead, journaling about your authenticity is a powerful step toward alignment. Meditations and guided meditations that change your neural pathways will also shift your external reality in a tangible way, whereas positive thinking and affirmations, in my experience, will not. And, building more simplicity, stability, stillness, and surrender into your day-to-day can create more energetic space for money to flow in because, contrary to popular belief, simplicity is not scarcity; in fact, simplicity is a close cousin of abundance.

Any challenge—whether financial, relational, health related—is a gift in disguise. In fact, the greater the challenge, the greater the gift. I firmly believe that the universe doesn't send us challenges, darkness, grief, or outright, full-on, total life crises unless it has something more aligned in store for us. In those moments of crisis, we are brought to our knees. We have to surrender, and we have to reach for the light. And in reaching for the light, we are forced to let go. We are forced to clear our neurological junk. We are forced to give over our imbalanced habits, relationships, and careers. We are forced to clean out our closets—our physical closets as well as our mental, emotional, and spiritual ones. And we are forced to grow because the pain of staying stuck is simply unbearable in those darkest moments.

The endgame of all this inner work, all this crisis-fueled growth? It's peace, joy, and love. And after all, isn't that what we really want when we are calling in money? We want the money to support the peace, the joy, and the love in our lives. Too often, money is associated with fear, stress, worry, punishment, oppression, control, and power. Those are not emotions of alignment, and these energies do not represent the truth about money. The truth is that, at the end of the day, we are all divine beings just trying to find our way home. Home is light and love. It's peace and joy. And the closer you move to those realities, the more the money will backfill to buoy those energies in your life.

To your abundance and your light.

APPENDIX

Grab a pen and paper and write down some answers to each one of these ten questions. Don't censor yourself or answer based on what you think you *should* want, what would make you a "good person," or what you would want your friends and family to see. This is for your eyes only, so be 100 percent true to yourself, even if it feels superficial, shameful, embarrassing, selfish, or silly.

1. Look around your home or office. What are the physical things around you? What are the first three types of physical things you see when you look around?
2. When you think about how you spend your time, what are the top three things you spend time on?
3. What are the three things that energize you the most?
4. What are the three things or categories of things you spend your money on most? The things you always find money for and would never cut out?
5. What are the three most organized areas of your life?
6. What are the three areas in which you're most reliable, disciplined, and focused? Where are you

---

1. Taken from Dr. John Demartini's Value Determination Process, which can be found at https://www.drdemartini.com.

most self-motivated? What do you never forget to do?

7. When you go down an internet rabbit hole, what are the three things you are most likely to explore?

8. If someone gave you $30,000 to give to charity, which three charities would be at the top of your list?

9. When you're talking with other people in casual or social settings, what are the top three things you most want to talk about? What are the top three conversation topics you find most interesting and engaging?

10. Who are the top three people or organizations that inspire you the most?

Look at your answers and consider this question: What are the four biggest themes that you see? Write them down and add some reflection about what each theme means to you.

For example, one of your four themes might be "beauty." Elaborate on what that means for you—maybe something like "being surrounded by nature and spending time in beautiful, undeveloped places." Or it could be something like "having beautiful clothes, hair, makeup, and nails and living in a gorgeous home with luxury furniture and a clean, modern style."

If you're feeling stuck or are having trouble seeing your four big themes, here are some examples of what other people have discovered and written with this exercise.

1. Health and wellness—meditating, eating well, moving, sleeping well, spending time in nature

2. Freedom—doing what I want, when I want, directing my life, and controlling my time

3. Intellect—reading, studying, and learning new things, sharing ideas
4. Relationships—spending time with my family and friends

or

1. Security—feeling safe, grounded, and cared for
2. Children—spending time with my kids and being there to support them
3. Travel—exploring new places and cultures, having adventures and new experiences
4. Community—being surrounded by people, connecting with others

ACKNOWLEDGMENTS

Nathaniel Hagood—Constancy, Joy, Adventure

Oliver Hagood—Nonconformity, Strength, Innovation

Cruz, the cockapoo—Loyalty, Tenderness, Cuddles

Marilyn Richey—Creativity, Beauty, Optimism

Jay Richey—Patience, Equanimity, Devotedness

Joanne Hyder—Music, Water, Friendship

Shannon Azzato Stephens—Fierceness, Kindness,
Thoroughness

Sara Spees Addicott—Support, Vision, Realization

ABOUT THE AUTHOR

Diana Richey is a financial planner and tax lawyer with over two decades of experience. She has worked with individuals and represented multinational corporations for everything from sustainable investing to international tax planning to charitable giving. She earned a BA with honors from the University of Chicago and a JD, cum laude, from Boston University School of Law. She is a certified financial planner (CFP®) and a trained mediator.

She lives in Jackson Hole, Wyoming, with her husband, son, and dog.